To Bud,
Thanks for your
love & support of our
military. Hope you enjoy
the book.
        Chaplain Sheri Snively

HEAVEN
IN THE
MIDST OF HELL

It was the best of times, it was the worst of times,
it was the age of wisdom, it was the age of foolishness,
it was the epoch of belief, it was the epoch of incredulity, it was the
season of Light, it was the season of Darkness, it was the spring of hope, it was
the winter of despair, we had everything before us, we had nothing before us,
we were all going direct to heaven, we were all going direct the other way—
in short, the period was so far like the present period, that some of its
noisiest authorities insisted on its being received, for good or for evil,
in the superlative degree of comparison only.

— CHARLES DICKENS,
A Tale of Two Cities

Mama is mad. Mama is sad. No one really knows why. "Tttt . . . Ttt . . . Ttt" rang out and jolted the silence. For an instant it sounded like short-burst rounds of automatic weapon fire. I turned toward the sound. "Knock it off!" I shouted. My two boys laughed and giggled. "No, I mean it," I said. "It's not funny." They tried their best to suppress their giggles and match my growing frown as their reflexive groans filled the air: "Aaah . . ." They were just playing a friendly game of war. But they knew an unexpected truce had been unilaterally called and enforced, so the young warriors frolicked off, maybe to a new game, maybe not. Their war may well have continued out of Mama's sight, but for now Mama is tired of playing war.

"Aaah . . ." The warriors groaned and grimaced as they gave voice to their pain. Day after day, gunshots and blasts provided a steady stream of blood across the steely, gray-green floor, and the pungent odor of burned flesh hung heavy in the warm air. This is a tale written while at war living between two cities, between Ramadi and Fallujah, where I served as the trauma hospital and mortuary affairs chaplain at Al Taqqadum in the heart of Al Anbar province, about sixty-five miles northwest of Baghdad.

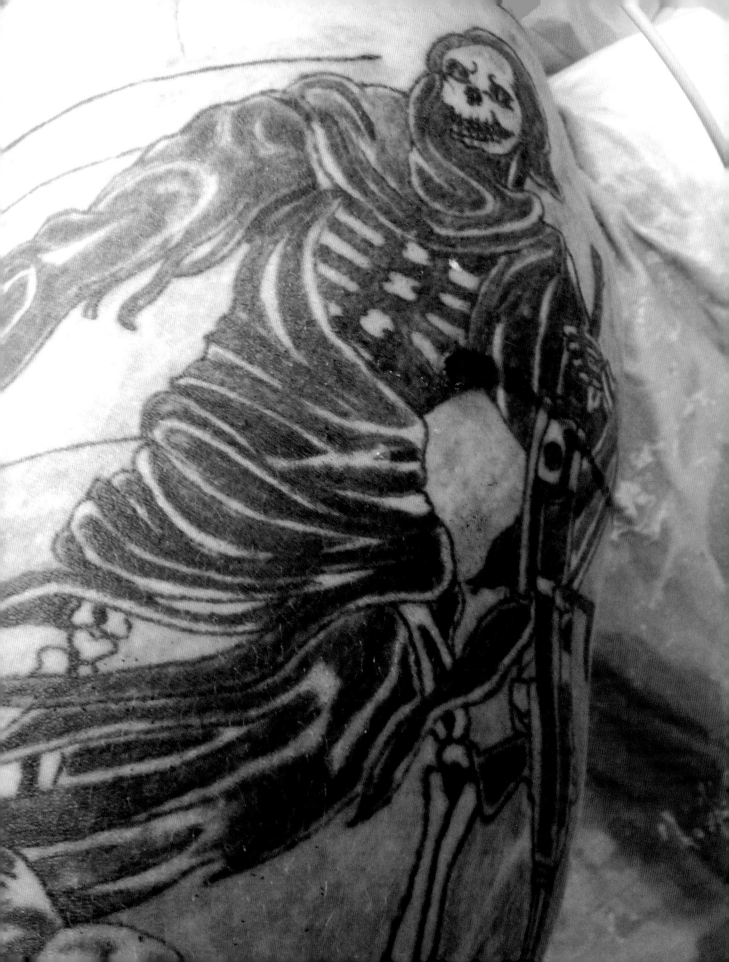

RAVEN OAKS
PRESS
SAN DIEGO, CALIFORNIA

HEAVEN
IN THE
MIDST OF HELL

A Quaker Chaplain's View
of the War in Iraq

STORIES AND PHOTOGRAPHS BY

Commander Sheri Snively, D.Min., CHC, USNR

FOREWORD BY

General James N. Mattis, USMC

Published by Raven Oaks Press
P.O. Box 1134 • Jamul, California, 91935 • 619.669.6552 • www.ravenoakspress.com

Produced by BookStudio, LLC
www.bookstudiobooks.com

Edited by Terence Spohn
Book design and layout by Charles McStravick, Artichoke Design

Printed in Korea

Publisher's Cataloging-in-Publication Data

Snively, Sheri.

Heaven in the midst of hell : a Quaker chaplain's view of the war in
Iraq / stories and photographs by Sheri Snively ; foreword by James
N. Mattis. -- 1st ed. -- Jamul, Calif. : Raven Oaks Press, c2010.

p. ; cm.

ISBN: 978-0-9819926-0-0
Includes index.

1. Iraq War, 2003- --Chaplains--Biography. 2. United States.
Marine Corps--Chaplains--Biography. 3. Iraq War, 2003- --
Personal narratives, American. 4. Society of Friends--United
States--Clergy--Biography. 5. Iraq War, 2003- --Pictorial works.
I. Title.

DS79.76 .S65 2010   2009930624
956.7044/37092--dc22   1004

CONTENTS

Personnel Retrieval and Processing (PRP) Marines outside the morgue at Al Taqqadum on the day
General Mattis came to visit. General Mattis, Chaplain Snively and RP3 Foreman are also in the picture.
PRP Marines are all reservists called to active duty during war time.

FOREWORD

EVERY MAN OR WOMAN'S WAR IS DIFFERENT. Serving in different units or locations, even in the same theater, means that every person going to war encounters their own personal reality. Each individual also brings their own perspective, as seen in this surprising book written by Sheri Snively, a Quaker Navy Chaplain assigned to a Marine Combat Service Support Group in Iraq's volatile Al Anbar Province. "Surprising" because of her Quaker background and the reality that she was a novice at war, she writes unlike many to whom war's grim realities are commonplace.

In this highly personal account and using her keen eye for detail, Chaplain Snively gracefully and insightfully gives a vivid account of her war. She brings the reader to her Iraq—the Sunni Triangle in a tumultuous time, in the midst of fighting before its Sunni population had turned against the enemy and made common cause with the American troops there. She honestly confronts her own thoughts and fears and provides a riveting window into the human side of war, a reality that can bludgeon the spirits of those who are part of it.

With her unique background and perspective, she provides a view of war that defies categorization, uncaptured by political ideology and focused on the human beings she comes to know in this very personal journey. She writes with an awareness that many veterans achieve only many years after their wartime experience, if they ever do. With her pacifist Quaker traditions often wrestling within the Marine Corps' warrior culture, she came to her own understanding, one that she shares openly and honestly, and one worth considering by those who also wish to understand.

— **JAMES N. MATTIS**
General, U.S. Marine Corps

PREFACE

"**G**O EASY ON YOURSELF and on others. No one wakes up in the morning, looks in the mirror, and says, 'How can I really screw up today?'"

General James Mattis encouraged us with words of wisdom when he came to visit Al Taqqadum. Far from an invitation to slack off, it was a recognition that we were all in Iraq together trying to do the best job we could. The message acknowledged the need to love and care for ourselves and the people around us in the midst of difficult circumstances. It was a profound truth known and expressed by warriors throughout the ages that the battle, and the war, is won by individuals. Ultimately that entails balance in life. Winning starts with each one of us working hard and being our best in mind, body, and spirit.

I had the opportunity to listen to General Mattis several times. He had an interesting message and an uncanny way of connecting with people throughout the ranks, from the lowest to the highest. I was impressed listening to this general who rose through the infantry ranks, a place not stereotypically known for its connection with the touchy-feely stuff! I smiled as he recalled his national fame several years ago when he was quoted out of context about killing people. He had a number of other colorful stories to tell. He made us laugh. That would have been memorable enough, but there was more to come.

It was lunchtime, and General Mattis saw me sitting alone in the chow hall. He left his entourage and came over. We must have talked for at least twenty minutes and covered many topics. He asked a lot of questions. "How are my guys really doing?" He discovered I was a Quaker minister and followed on by asking, "How are you doing? This must be very difficult for you. . . ." He continued his encouragement and admonition to me. "You have a unique perspective that needs to be heard. Are you writing this down? You need to write this down."

Thank you, General Mattis. I was capturing some of it already, but I took your words to heart, took them as an order, and worked even harder on my journalistic mission when I got home. So here is the result: a collection of stories from Iraq, told through the perspective of a female Quaker minister and U.S. Navy chaplain serving with U.S. Marines in a combat zone.

GETTING THERE

OLD WARRIOR
WISDOM

"DO YOU SING?" HE ASKED. I must have given him a funny look in response because he continued. "No, really, you need to know some of the standard hymns and the Twenty-third Psalm. Do you know that by heart? You need to know that, too."

We moved around the dance floor to a slow but happy 1940s love song, music from our parents' era. John, a Vietnam-era Navy SEAL who was there with his dad, was giving me words of wisdom, last-minute advice before I entered the combat zone. My departure date was only a few days away.

"It won't be easy, but you'll do fine. You'll be mother, sister, lover all in one for those guys." His expression changed. He had a funny look on his face and a strange look in his eye as he paused. It was obvious he was thinking carefully about his next comments. One happy song gave way to the next. He pulled me closer and held me tight. He looked me in the eyes and his eyes welled with tears as he said, "I've had guys die in my arms. Some silently slip away, some scream for their mothers. You'll hear their screams and you'll wear their blood."

I danced with many that night. It was a perfect sendoff. The Silver Eagles (World War II U.S. Navy enlisted pilots) were gathered in San Diego for their annual reunion. The timing couldn't have been better. I was lost in the magic of the moment. It was a room full of seventy or eighty guys just like my daddy. He is no longer here and could not send me to war, but these guys were here and could. My daddy had known a few of these guys personally; they'd been in the same squadrons and had flown together. The connection with them always gave me a warm and cozy feeling. I'm happy to be their chaplain at the San Diego Wing and for the national organization. It's always fun to be with them, to sit and to listen to their stories and to laugh at their jokes. Tonight was no different, but then again it was very different and we all knew it. I wondered what lay ahead. They knew. They'd been there—not to Iraq, but they'd been to war and back.

> **WARM EMBRACES WERE SPRINKLED WITH LAUGHTER AND TEARS. I WANTED TO GO AND SERVE AND THEY KNEW IT.**

One by one around the banquet tables, at the bar and on the dance floor, the Silver Eagles gave me words of wisdom, advice, and blessing. Some couldn't even speak. It was too emotional. They just looked at me and their eyes welled with tears. They squeezed me tight and then just stared at me for a long, long time. Finally they shook their heads and wiped the tears rolling down their cheeks. I don't know whether it was because they were remembering their own war horrors or because they were imagining the horrors that awaited me. It was probably some of both. My initiation lay ahead; they knew first hand what I did not know yet.

Chaplain Snively with Bob Dunham, a former Navy enlisted pilot from World War II during the Silver Eagle reunion in San Diego, California, October 2006.

Warm embraces were sprinkled with laughter and tears. I wanted to go and serve, and they knew it. They supported my deployment like fellow Naval and Marine Corps buddies or like patriotic Americans. They were proud the way any dad would be, but it was still hard to say that final good-bye. We lingered a long time that night, not sure whether we would ever see each other again. Not only could I be killed, but it was likely that because of age or health problems, some of them would die before I got home. But it was finally time, after one last drink, one last dance, one last embrace, one last good-bye; the old warriors wrapped me in a warm blanket of love and blessing and sent me to war.

The music stopped and the lights came up. John still held me close and whispered to me, *"Sing and pray. Hold them, hug them, love them!"* I wiped the tears from my eyes as my gaze met his and whispered a promise in return: "I will."

يقاتلون معك
من أجل أن تعيشوا بسلام

FIGHTING TOGETHER
TO LIVE IN PEACE

SWEARING AND KNIFE FIGHTING

"**H**OWYA DOIN' THIS MORNING?**" the gas station attendant asked as he looked up from behind the cash register. I sighed, put the cold bottle of water on the counter, and responded, "I'm okay. But a little tired and harried. I'm getting ready for a trip and I'm not done packing. Got a lot to do today and I've got some long days ahead of me." He nodded, turned his attention to the water, and scanned the bar code. He also looked at the cash register and out the window at the cars at the gas pumps. He was doing everything that needed to be done all at once, multi-tasking at its finest. Obviously dedicated to good customer service he took cues from me, made friendly conversation, and asked, "So where are you going?" I stopped digging through my purse trying to find correct change, looked at him and answered, "I'm going to Iraq."

He stared at me in disbelief. Now I had his full and undivided attention. A jumble of statements and questions spontaneously poured from him. "What in the hell are you going there for? I'm from there and I wouldn't be there now. I left there fifteen years ago, haven't been back since. You don't want to go there. You're not really going there, are you? What in the world do you do?"

I quickly explained, "I'm a Navy chaplain serving with Marines." Still shaking his head in disbelief he offered his help. "Well, I'll teach you some words and phrases. What do you want to know how to say? I'll write them down for you and you can pick them up in couple days and learn them before you go. When do you leave?" "Thanks for the offer." I said. "It's a great idea. Unfortunately I leave really early tomorrow morning. I have to be at the airport before six." He shook his head again. "Man, that's too early—we open at six but you'll already be gone, too bad. But how 'bout I teach you something right now? What do you want to know how to say?" I had no idea and so I put the question back to him. "What do you think I need to know? Maybe something that is not on my Arabic tapes or in the books. Slang might be useful." "Hmm," he pondered out loud. He thought about it for a minute and then said, "Okay, I've got it. This is good. If you ever need to use it they won't expect it, especially from the chaplain. The shock value will be worth a lot."

He repeated a phrase over and over. He had me do the same. I wasn't getting it. Arabic is so different. He needed to write it down so I could see it phonetically. Neither of us had any paper. He looked around and said, "Here we go. This will work." He ripped a piece of receipt paper from the cash register and carefully wrote the phrase. I read it slowly and cautiously at first, "Ebin el ga haba." I still didn't know what he was teaching me or what I was saying. Intuitively I knew it wasn't very "chaplainly." He had me repeat it over and over. He was very encouraging, smiled, and said, "Good. That's better. Now just add the speed and punch to it. You have to say it with power. Say it like you mean it." I was more than a little self-conscious, trying to pronounce very foreign sounding words and realizing, too, that now some of the only Arabic words I knew were swear words. But I must have done okay because my newfound Chaldean friend, Mike, smiled and gave the pronouncement, "You've got it. You're ready to go. Come by and see me when you get back. I want to know how it goes." I smiled too, yes I was ready. I reached out and hugged him. "Thanks. Thanks for your help. I'll let you know how it goes."

Wonderful! The swear words were sure to go well with the two hours of hand-to-hand combat knife training provided me earlier that morning by my Tae Kwon Do Grand Master and former Vietnam Army Ranger friend. He too was helping me get ready with last-minute training and last-minute words of wisdom. It was the perfect combination; now I had words to yell at an opponent in a knife fight.

I STILL DIDN'T KNOW WHAT HE WAS TEACHING ME OR WHAT I WAS SAYING. INTUITIVELY I KNEW IT WASN'T VERY "CHAPLAINLY."

The reality was, however, if I had to get close enough to a bad guy to use a knife or yell swear words, I was in deep trouble and something had gone terribly wrong. It would mean I was in the wrong place at the wrong time without my body guard (chaplains do not carry weapons) and my Marines nowhere to be found. Quite frankly, I knew if I were to find myself in that situation in a war zone I'd be screwed probably both literally and figuratively. I tried not to think about those possibilities. I knew the required "what to do if you become a prisoner of war" pre-deployment training was feeding my ove-active imagination.

There was a certain twisted humor in my knife training and crash language course. It made me smile. On the other hand, *I knew in my heart I could never use my newfound skills.* They were 180 degrees opposite of my calling of connecting with compassion and living in love. But I learned eagerly and accepted the gifts with thanksgiving. I knew these guys cared. They were sharing their time and their talents with me, preparing me and trying to insure that I survived and came home. Hour by hour I was getting closer. In the days and weeks to come I knew I would think of these guys and other friends and strangers who helped me get ready. I would remember and smile.

THE GARDEN OF EDEN

"The cradle of civilization" is the academic term. The phrase conjures images of an ancient land rich in history, rich in tradition, and rich in wisdom. The Garden of Eden is the religious term; the phrase conjures images of peace and plenty, of an abundant and verdant land, of a people at one with each other and their God. In Iraq, regardless of the term one chose, there were times when some of us would wonder out loud together, "What happened?" Somebody robbed the cradle. Somebody sprayed a potent herbicide in the garden.

One might argue over the exact location, maybe a few hundred miles south, but many agree on the general locale: the place where the Tigris and Euphrates Rivers meet. We wondered what it was like. It must have been beautiful.

I made it my job to look for those remnants of heaven in the midst of hell.

We lived on a seemingly godforsaken, barren desert plateau above one of the rivers, above one of the lakes. It could have been a pretty place. I think it used to be. There were indeed hints here and there. You had to look pretty hard, though—the clues were well hidden. We were newcomers to the area but even the locals seemed to have forgotten. I wondered whether it might be like other ancient places degraded by years of neglect, covered by the drifting desert sand, and lost through the years, only waiting and hoping to be discovered and treasured by some future generation. Were there secrets waiting to be unlocked, understood, and unleashed? I think so, but I think the signs are subtle, nearly

imperceptible; they are easy to overlook. Most people didn't bother to look anymore. Indeed, it was hard to see beyond the monotony of desert-sand brown. It was hard to see beyond the death and destruction. It was hard to hear the birds sing above the roar of the generators. It was hard to see beyond day-to-day existence. It's hard to think about paradise past, to wonder about ancient secrets and wisdom or the promised dawn of a new day, and paradise future when the present is a never-ending purgatory, a never-ending cycle of violence and the struggle to survive.

We took our turn tending the devastated garden. We talked as we tended. We wondered out loud together and had lots of questions but very few answers. What happened to this place where human history began?

CHANCE
CONVERSATIONS

I'D JOINED THE NAVY, NOT THE CIRCUS. But now I was juggling bags that were too big and too heavy for any normal human being to carry. We all were—eight Marines and me. Bags jumped off the carts with a mind of their own. They rolled onto the floor almost as if cued by an unseen ringmaster. I struggled to get mine back in place and then pleaded with them as if they understood and wanted to cooperate. I muttered a prayer under my breath, "Oh please, just a little bit more, hang in there . . ." And just in case that didn't work, I threw in a command: "Dammit, stay there!" Something had to work. I was on the verge of laughing. I was on the verge of crying. It was funny. It was exasperating. It was just a taste of the months to come, when events would prompt me to laugh or cry or do both at the same time. Little by little, we made our way across the Baltimore terminal from the regular passenger area to where we would catch the rotator to Germany and beyond. My weightlifting and running had helped; at least I was keeping up with my Marines.

I patted my bags in praise, as if they were loyal furry companions. The bags didn't have a tail to wag, nor did they smile or slobber at me in response. I remembered my marginal success in training dogs. That wasn't a good sign. Bag training might go better, but I wasn't sure. Bags don't have brains, but their mischievous and unruly personalities emerged. Yet the Marines had an extra piece of gear I did not; they juggled their weapons, too.

We were quite a sight. Nine of us, eight Marines and me, walked in civilian clothes down the passageways of the airport, each with a little shopping cart full of gear: green sea bags and digital backpacks stuffed nearly to overflowing, and in each Marine's bag an M-16. Going to war in years past was never like this. Stares from people all around confirmed that.

One man couldn't help but comment, "Wow, that's not how we got over to Vietnam during my time. Hey, good luck, and you all come back safe." He shook our hands, smiled, waved, and watched us walk away. He recognized the magnitude of our task and gave us what he could, his blessing. It was a brief exchange between one who'd been there and ones who soon would be; he knew as we would soon know. Some things never change. War is war; things get broken and people get hurt or killed. People know that instinctively; veterans know it in reality.

> IN WAR EVERYTHING
> IS MAGNIFIED.
> THE PAIN IS DEEPER.
> THE JOY IS SWEETER.
> THE BIG QUESTIONS OF LIFE
> SEEM MORE URGENT
> BUT LESS ANSWERABLE.

A Vietnam vet named Lawrence sat next to me on the flight to Baltimore. He saw the irony in my situation. "Wow, I'm going home after a nice conference in San Diego and you're going off to war. You know, with a few of the guys on this flight you can tell by their haircuts, but wow, I would never have known about you unless you told me. I remember how alone I felt going to Vietnam . . . alone and scared . . . and I was on a flight with all military people. It must be strange for you to be truly alone, or with just a few other Marines you've never met." Going to war alone is an odd and increasing reality for many serving in the Navy as individual augmentees and reservists. It was nice to have someone recognize the increased challenge of going it alone.

My seatmate and I talked a little politics: the similarities and differences between Vietnam and Iraq. We talked about his life post-Vietnam. Most eventually returned from the war. Life goes on and life is good, but one is forever changed. He's had a pretty good life, but it has been marked by a forty-year struggle with post-traumatic stress disorder. I wondered about this generation, and more specifically my guys and me, as no one is immune from the effects of war. We talked a long time about many things. Finally he concluded, "There are no accidents, so I don't take it lightly that you sat next to me. Thank you. You've helped me deepen what I've learned in the last three or four months. You'll do fine in Iraq. I'd love to know how it goes for you."

I sensed that these conversations, on airplanes and in the airports, were the last pep talks before the big game. I had trained hard and spent a lifetime preparing. I was ready and I knew it. But total strangers, Vietnam veterans who received so little support, reached out and encouraged and blessed me, saying, "You have what it takes to make it. You'll make it. But more than that you have what it takes to help others in the midst of confusion and chaos."

Meeting them confirmed other things for me as well. I knew that whether on the way to war or coming home from war, whether it's four days, four months, or forty years post-deployment, the issues, the questions, and the struggles remain the same. "Good" wars or bad, popular or unpopular, win or lose, wars pose deep and difficult questions and leave scars on the body, mind, and spirit. Many who participate up close and personally continue in a battle the rest of their lives. It is easy to see God when things are going well, but part of the spiritual path, a place of deeper wisdom, power, and peace, is to stand in awe and recognize the Divine everywhere, even in the midst of desolation and despair.

My airplane seatmate reminded me to think about these things, not just for my own sake but for the sake of those I serve. I needed to think about deeper things. I needed to continue meditation and prayer and continue to practice letting go and going with the flow. In war everything is magnified. The pain is deeper. The joy is sweeter. The big questions of life seem more urgent but less answerable. The paradoxes of life are more striking and more puzzling. Wanting total control and being able to let go are opposites that exist simultaneously. Part of the human struggle is to make sense of and balance the need for power and control against the freedom and peace that comes with letting go. Most of the time we contemplate this and other questions from the relative safety of our own neatly ordered little world; war changes that.

In war, heightened situational awareness and control of the battle space help ensure positive outcomes. Yet it quickly becomes apparent that no one, no unit, no matter how well trained, can control everything. There are too many variables and there are always unknowns and surprises. Sometimes it works to your advantage; other times it costs you everything. We've all heard the stories of people inexplicably, miraculously saved from destruction while others were unexpectedly disfigured, disabled, or killed when they weren't "supposed" to have been. I would soon see those people and hear the stories first hand. Control what you can and let the rest go: an important place to reach in everyday life, even more so in war. More than sheer determination and beyond resignation, courage and acceptance come from trust, a true letting go. Only when one comes to that inner point of love and peace is all fear truly gone. Perhaps my journey to Iraq would take me to that place too.

I had a window seat. Landing in Baltimore, as far as the eye could see there was a fiery glow. Was it sunrise? Was it sunset? Was it a wildfire? It was late afternoon, but it looked like the sunset had gotten an early start. The trees were a beautiful multitude of reds, oranges, and yellows, every shade and hue in the warm palette. The trees were like a vibrant garden of fall flowers created not from blossoms but from leaves. It was like a plush red carpet rolled out in welcome.

The fall leaves would be one of my last sights of home for awhile. It could be one of the last views of home forever. Everybody thinks they'll come home. But who knows? There are no guarantees, not even for a chaplain. We are not immune from the sights, the sounds, the smells of war, neither are we immune from devastation and death. I tried not to think about it too much, but I was going to the real thing; this was the real deal. Real people were suffering and dying and I was going to join them. I was going into the belly of the beast; some would say I was going to visit hell.

The evening shadows grew longer. Nature knew she looked smashing and flirted with anyone willing to appreciate her beauty. So I savored the sights. I knew the vibrant, warm, deep red of fall leaves was more soothing and peaceful than the deep, warm, blood red I was about to see. I wanted to remember the leaves. They encouraged and blessed me. Who knows what the trees would be like when I got home? They might be stark naked and exposed to the winter chill or they might be just budding out in springtime finery. Or by then, they might be clothed in a full canopy of green, a quiet place of refuge from intense summer sun or a shady place of respite from the memories of a stark desert half a world away. I wondered what it would look like flying into Iraq. Would there even be any trees?

My preparation and spiritual journey taught me, and my airplane seatmates and airport conversations reconfirmed, that chance conversations and heart connections were all around, just waiting to be found. They might be hidden, but blessings abound. I knew there would be encouraging conversations, blessings from people and blessings everywhere in Iraq: from the trees, the sunsets, unexpected people and places. Intuitively I knew these would be the hints of heaven in the midst of hell.

SURROUNDED BY PRAYER

The Tibetan Buddhist prayer flags fluttered in the breeze: red, yellow, green, blue, white—simple, small square pieces of cloth. Each one filled with inscriptions: pictures and words from a culture and in a language I did not understand. I trusted intuitively that they were helping words. I trusted that they were pictures of helping deities. And I knew that I could use any help I could get. I was not standing on ceremony nor was I limiting my options. I was open and receptive to prayers given and received from all sources for me and my people.

Although not a part of my own tradition, I knew the concept of the prayer flag. If nothing else, I'd seen pictures and read an article about them in *National Geographic*. Faithful followers write prayers on small pieces of colored cloth and tie them outside to blow freely in the breeze. The wind catches the flag and catches the prayers, too, and carries the request aloft with the hope of heaven hearing and responding.

I was busy working. I was busy relaxing. I was sometimes busy eating and sleeping and working out. In short, I was doing the stuff of everyday life in Iraq. But no matter what I was doing, it gave me comfort to know I was surrounded by prayer. Beside my twin bed made up with blue checkered Disney *Cars* sheets was my bedstand, a second-, third-, or even fourth-hand hand-me-down table turned makeshift altar. A small Shiva idol, a mercy Buddha, a rosary, a cross, a few sacred stones gathered from Hawaii, Memphis, and Chicago, and encouraging words written on small scraps of paper all combined to form a circle of ongoing prayer. My Tibetan prayer flags were busy praying, too. They sent forth petitions day and night, blown vigorously 24/7 by the air conditioner/heater unit in my little 10x20-foot trailer room number E15, just off the main drag behind the concrete blast barriers at Al Taqqadum's mainside.

MORNING
AND EVENING
THE FIRST DAY

IT WAS MORNING of the first day. The early dawn light broke through scattered clouds. There was a touch of pink and yellow, almost as if it had been painted on the few clear patches on the gray, drizzly sky. There was only a hint of the hidden sun. A few drops of rain fell. A brown songbird landed at the peak of the brown tent and sang its morning song. It all brought renewal and hope to the new day. We needed some refreshment about now. We were briefly under the care of the Army, O-6 to lance corporal standing side by side for muster at 0500 in the cold rain having traveled nonstop for two or three days, and we still were not at our final destination. Yes, indeed, we could use some refreshment. Anything would be welcome: food, rest, or a shower. For the moment, however, we would have to be satisfied with the hint of sunshine on a rainy day and a little brown bird saying, "Hello, welcome to Kuwait."

It was evening of the first day. The sunset was equally as inviting and renewing for anyone paying attention. But most were probably just too tired to notice. We had spent the day waiting and wondering when we'd go. Now it was obvious; dusk was at hand. There was a hazy, misty brown spreading across the horizon. It was getting dark. No one noticed the emerging sky show, and I really didn't have time to enjoy it right then either. We were busy moving gear and catching a bus to take us to yet another flight. Once settled into the "bus stop," however, I looked around and saw the gorgeous full moon. What a delightful sight for my first night in the Middle East! I knew she would be present with me in the days to come. The moon is so feminine: a subtle, constant, and gentle presence. Giving light but not overpowering, she wants to be noticed and adored but never demands it. She looked over all the Marines standing there, but I don't think any of them noticed her until I pointed out her beauty. One said in response, "Hmm, it might not be such a great night to fly . . . all lit up, you know." Yes, I guess that just shows the amazing reality of stark contrasts and paradoxes that exist simultaneously. I see beauty, and he sees planning and maneuver. But really both of us can see both sides, and in order to survive Iraq we must!

I thought again about where I was. I was about to be in the middle of "It": the place you always read about, the place you always see on TV, the mess in the Middle East. This is the real deal. I'm on my way to war. It was evident. I thought about riding in the very large, very targetable bus convoy from the airport and now back again. We were accompanied by plain-clothed security and Marines with weapons at the ready. They enforced blackout conditions on the bus: no lights on, no peeking out the curtained windows. I must admit that I sneaked a peak once or twice. But I felt safe. I guess that was good, and I guessed it was good, too, that the reality was beginning to sink in. This was not a drill.

It is thrilling, exciting, and wonderful to be here surrounded by my Marines, the modern-day warriors. I love them and they love me. The Marines I traveled with from San Diego watched out for me and showed me the buddy system in action. I think they understood and appreciated that I didn't "have" to be there. I chose to go to war. More than just a volunteer in the all-volunteer Navy, I asked for the orders to Iraq. One Marine expressed his thank you this way: "I don't know, I just feel better about having a 'holy'

Good co-workers and a positive, professional atmosphere is important in any workplace, even more so in a difficult, deployed environment. The Al Taqqadum Main side Religious Ministries Team (RMT) supported each other so we in turn could support the soldiers, sailors, airmen, marines and civilians under our care. From left to right: RPC Bernardo, Chaplain Hunt, RP3 Foreman, Chaplain Spencer, RP2 McCormick, and Chaplain Snively.

person around." I protested the label "holy," at least as it's commonly used, and said, "Well, maybe I'm someone who reminds you to connect spiritually and maybe tries to do so more than others. But you know you don't need me. You can do that for each other." He nodded and smiled and said, "Yeah, but we don't. That's why we need you. Thanks for coming." What a wonderful reminder of what we can do for each other, and an amazingly succinct statement of what my role is among them! Although we were weary and had a fair amount of anticipation of what was to come, it was a great first day.

It was morning and it was evening of the first night. We boarded a C-130, left Kuwait, and began our final leg of the journey, a journey that would affect and change us forever. Well after midnight we landed in Iraq. It was early morning of the second day.

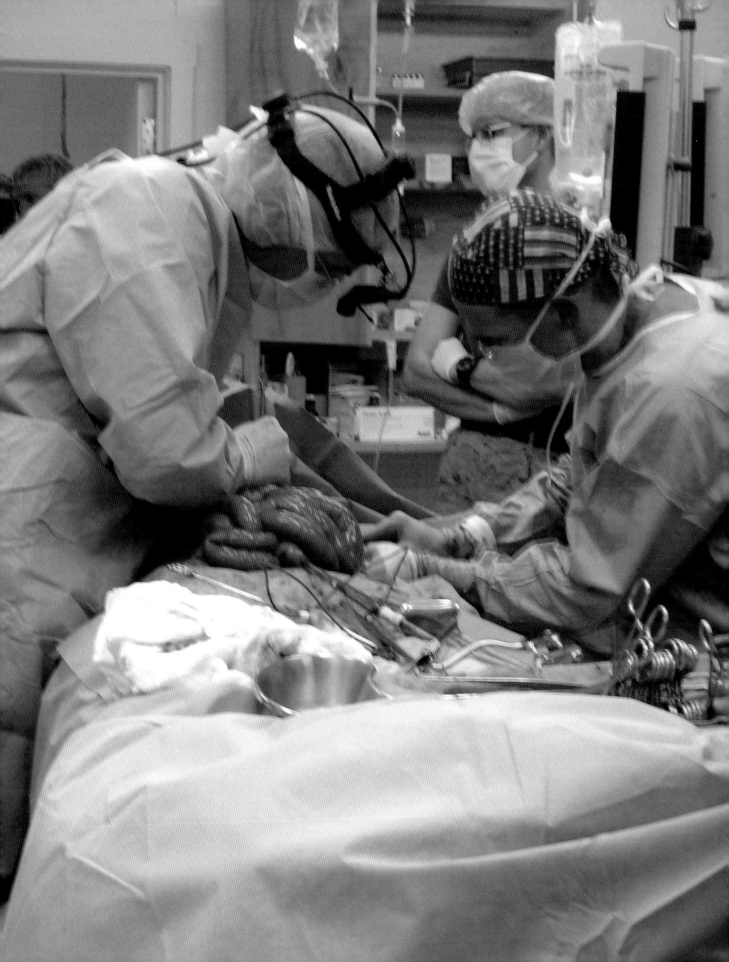

THE TRAUMA
ROOM

"**W**E HAVE TO STOP MEETING LIKE THIS," she said in a serious tone.

I nodded my head and said quietly, "Yeah, you're right, but I don't think we have much say about it, do we?"

"No, apparently not, but have you noticed every time we've been on-call together the last couple months we've gotten the really bad cases?" The supervising nurse was right. We'd attended some awful trauma cases together.

A pleasant Sunday afternoon had turned into one of the worst. We received two severely injured patients struggling to survive, the result of a law-enforcement helicopter crash in East San Diego County. For one patient the struggle was over quickly. He died in the trauma room as surgeons worked diligently and furiously to stabilize him for further surgery and repair. The officer's leg dangled by a thread and his matching arm was severed, sheared off in the accident. It lay in a plastic bag across the room.

The nurse and I moved out of the trauma room and talked with a few law-enforcement officers, their chaplain, and the family. After the initial shock, the tears, the prayers, and heavy silence that descended on the scene, the family asked about the patient's personal effects: his ring and his watch. The nurse and I made our way back to the trauma room to look for them. As the medical team continued to clean up and document the case, we found the bag containing the severed arm. We were successful in our search. Attached to the bloody, lifeless arm were the wedding ring and watch. We slipped the ring off the finger and the watch from the wrist and cleaned them. The situation was beyond words. We gave each other one of those looks as our eyes welled with tears.

I WAS EXACTLY WHERE I WAS SUPPOSED TO BE.

Neither of us knew what to say. Finally I said, "Wow! These cases just keep getting harder. It makes me wonder what I am being prepared for in the future." I paused, sighed, and continued. "But I think I know. I'm a Navy Reserve chaplain serving with a Marine unit, so it is very likely that someday I could be with them somewhere seeing this and worse every day. No experience is ever wasted. I am being prepared for battle."

Ten years later I was working in another hospital halfway around the world. Less than twelve hours after landing in Iraq, I stood in another trauma room. The smell of warm, fresh blood, oil, fear, flesh burned by blasts, and flesh burned by cauterization filled the air and mingled in a bizarre mix of scents. The patient's leg dangled by a thread; the surgeons worked diligently and furiously to save him. It was too much. It was too late. He lost his leg. He lost his life, too.

My mind spun. My head reeled. My eyes welled with tears. It was nearly overwhelming: the sights, the sounds, the reality. But I was prepared in mind, body, and spirit. I was exactly where I was supposed to be. There was no place I would rather be. I was at war with my Marines.

THE WILD, WILD WEST

A 21ST-CENTURY WESTERN

THE BIG, BRIGHT SUN SANK SLOWLY in the western sky, casting a subtle glow across the clouds and creating a beautiful palette in shades of orange and pink. The fiery ball grew bigger and bigger as it neared the edge of the horizon, slipping steadily, silently from sight. A gentle breeze kissed the evening hello. The leaves on the trees responded to the teasing with a little quiver. The birds soared easily, almost playfully, in the early evening cool. The hustle and bustle of the street below was evident. The vehicles were large and small; some were in a hurry, some moved slowly. People walked along the edge of the road, bags in hand, heading home after a shopping trip. Others ran by, using the last light of the day to exercise outside, jogging along the road before dinnertime.

Most of the little town was visible from my rooftop patio perch. I sat enjoying it all: the view, a cool drink, the pleasant temperature, and a moment of relaxation in this little desert town. I thought about it: people pay big money for trips to a desert resort in the winter. I took it all in and sat savoring the moment, drinking deeply of the scene, etching the sights, the sounds, and the smells into my mind. It was the perfect place for an evening happy hour.

Well, on second thought, not quite perfect. There were a few noticeable flaws. As one looked around more closely, a few other details became apparent and quite frankly were a little concerning. Yes, I guess the old saying "the devil is in the details" is true.

I LIKE WESTERNS. MAYBE IT IS BECAUSE EVEN THOUGH LIFE WAS HARD, EVERYTHING SEEMED TO WORK OUT NEAT AND TIDY IN A ONE-HOUR SHOW.

Most all the vehicles were tan or green. Occasionally a white contractor/construction truck appeared on the road. Funny, I thought, even here the contractors drive white trucks. None of the roads were paved; they were all dirt and gravel. Nobody was moving very fast, but dust flew everywhere as the vehicles rumbled along. A boom box blasted its tunes for all to hear. It had to be loud inside the vehicle if I could hear it from where I sat. I guess every neighborhood has a few vehicles that run around town like that. Funny, though, I wasn't bothered by it; it actually made me smile. They were playing music I liked, good ol' rock and roll.

Acrid fumes from fires and diesel engines lingered and hung heavy in the air. It was probably better not to think of the health or environmental risks from the fires burning trash and who knows what else. Of course, the alternative of letting it build up was not acceptable either. It was hard to say which was the lesser of two evils, but that seems to be a recurring theme on many issues in these parts these days. Generators whirred and hummed a steady tune, almost hypnotic, almost irritating, but soothing in a strange sort of way. A steady pop, pop, pop could be heard over the monotonous droning of mechanical noise. A tangle of wires hung from poles, some still useful; most long ago lost their purpose but still remain and now obstruct the sunset view. Some of these things would make writing a real-estate ad more difficult, but with a little work and a little focus on the positives, this could be a charming place. In fact, it was a charming place even with its quirks and drawbacks. Many people

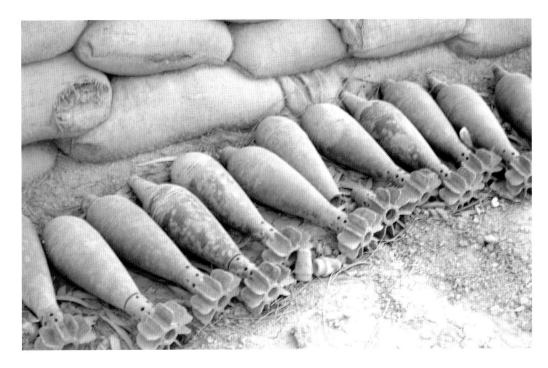

Not exactly the kind of souvenirs you want to find along the road. Old ordnance left over from another time, another war but was still deadly and useful to the insurgency until collected and disarmed by the EOD teams around Al Anbar Province.

complained about it. They had their reasons, many of which were valid and understandable. But I liked this little town set near the banks of the river.

The dust, the smoke, the smell, the wires, and even the pop, pop, pop—all that was relatively easy to ignore. So, too, were the deficiencies of my rooftop patio: the folding chair, the makeshift table, and nothing stronger than a cold diet 7-Up. But I made the best of it, finding a place of solace for reflection, to think about the previous few whirlwind weeks and what the future weeks might hold. It was a spiritual retreat in the midst of it all with my notebook and pen in hand, my camera, and my own thoughts. It was comfortable and relatively peaceful, until something happened that couldn't be ignored. There was a sudden kaboom, rattle, shake. Seven times . . . kaboom, rattle, shake. The peace of my rooftop sunset meditation was rocked. I was no expert (and still am not) on the subtleties of knowing when a kaboom, rattle, shake indicates incoming or outgoing. Was it artillery fire? Was it mortar or rocket fire? Was it us? Was it them? Suddenly the details didn't seem as important as the fact that my rooftop vantage point was close by the activity. I didn't feel as secure as I had five

minutes earlier, contemplating life and death, peace and war from a secure distance. Maybe the rooftop was not the safest place to be. But that, of course, begged the question: Was anywhere around here "safe"? I tried not to think about that reality and told myself I'd better check with someone who'd been around longer than I. Being a newcomer and a visitor in town, I was totally clueless. Later, I found out that most people just learn to ignore the kaboom, rattle, shake, because if it's incoming, by the time you hear it you're either hit or you're not. A few others actually run to rooftop vantage points to get a good view, to see what they can see. Of course, neither of those is the approved response.

Besides the rockets, mortar, artillery, or whatever it was, the other nagging reality tucked in my head was the warning about snipers in the area. I knew logically and felt relatively secure that my patio rooftop perch was far enough in the interior of the base. But who knew for sure? My mind started playing games with me. Anything was possible with a good rifle, a good shot, and a little luck. My personal rooftop-patio happy hour could offer a good target from outside the wire. But now the close proximity of the kaboom, rattle, shake was making me rethink my evening entertainment. I thought (probably because I wanted to believe) that the kaboom, rattle, shake was outgoing fire, not incoming. Nonetheless, my reasoning was that I should calmly "proceed to the exit" and decide on a new activity for the evening. The pop, pop, pop and the boom, boom, boom were not just background noise and sound effects on a fantasy stage set. This was the real deal.

And it was close by. This was no longer a time to contemplate a "gun battle" in theory. It was a reality that was demanding more immediate action. Perhaps I didn't need to contemplate right now nor watch the unfolding show. I also didn't need to unwittingly play a different part in the show other than my assigned role. I thought about the evacuation instructions given in certain situations that go something like, "Please remain calm and move quickly to the nearest exit." I kept repeating this phrase in my mind and executed my own instructions. My newfound mantra focused me and gave me something concrete to do. By the fourth kaboom, I was in the stairway at the other end of the building.

My drink and journal in hand, I left the chair on the roof, figuring it could be retrieved later. Just like on an airplane, in case of evacuation they tell you to leave the extraneous stuff behind so as not to encumber your movement. I couldn't move quickly with the chair in hand; I'd deal with it later. Appropriately or not, I stopped by the Combat Stress Office on my way down from the roof. There were two reasons: it was their chair; and their office door opened into the passageway near the stairs leading to the roof.

The psychiatrist gave me a crazy little smile. "So those blasts brought you down off the roof?" he stated as much as asked.

I gave a half-nervous, half-relieved laugh in return and said, "You're right."

He gave me a knowing look and went on to say, "I won't go up there at all. Too dangerous, way too dangerous; my intuition tells me, don't do it. Those snipers in town are good, you know?" He continued talking about the area, the place, the local happenings, his political leanings on the subject, and how he would "solve" the problem. I just nodded and tried to smile in response to his musings and crazy-eyed look. I was still thinking about the pop, pop, pop and the boom, boom, boom. It was closer here in Ramadi than I had experienced at "home" in Al Taqqadum about twenty-five miles away. Of course, I'd been in my new home for only about ten days, so I really didn't have much of a basis for comparison. But I went to bed that night lulled to sleep by a new lullaby: pop, pop, pop and boom, boom, boom. Recognizing with each pop and each boom that someone somewhere was likely getting killed.

As a kid, I watched black-and-white reruns of television shows like *Bonanza* and *Gunsmoke*. I like westerns. Maybe it is because I rode horses. Maybe it is because I was a pretty good shot with my .22 rifle. Maybe it is because my dad liked to watch westerns and I liked spending time with him. Maybe it is because even though life was hard, everything seemed to work out neat and tidy in a one-hour show. It was a strange connection, Iraq in November 2006 with the Wild West of the southwestern United States in the 1800s.

Jeff and I met in the Marine Corps Martial Arts Training Tent. He and I and a civilian contractor were the odd ones out (the only non-Marines), so we trained together every morning at 0800 for about an hour.

I am not the first to see the similarities. Al Anbar province has been called the Wild West. In a strange paradox, the gorgeous, colorful Ramadi sunset view from my rooftop patio indeed reminded me of the black-and-white western reruns. It looked and sounded like a town in the Wild West. In many ways it is. It was just like an old western television show or movie: dusty streets, good guys fighting bad guys in gun battles, and gossip galore that keeps the storyline of small-town life interesting. But it is a western with a twist. It is a twenty-first—century western. Instead of horses there are Humvees; instead of boots and chaps there are boots and flak; instead of .22s or .30/.30s there are M-16s. I just hope it ends like all good westerns do: the good guys win, the town is saved, children are safe to play in the streets again, shops open and do a thriving business, the hero gets the girl, and everyone lives happily ever after. Wouldn't that be nice?

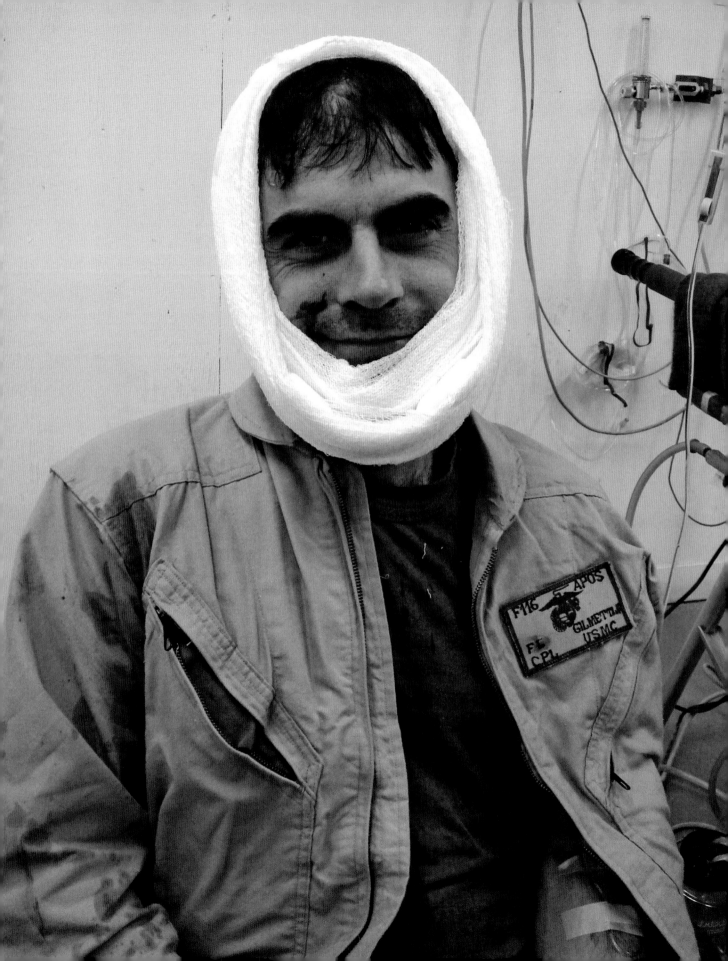

BEDSIDE WISDOM

"CHAPLAIN, HEY CHAPLAIN," the voice carried across the room. The Marine sitting in the emergency room saw me coming. I was happy for the greeting for many reasons. First, he was stable and awaiting further evaluation. All things considered, he was in good shape, and that was a good thing. There was time for conversation, and obviously something was on his mind. Second, most Marines appreciate their chaplains, and it's always nice to be appreciated. I smiled and waved a response as I approached. "Hey, what's up?"

One might think the questions posed to a chaplain in an ER would consist of issues about life and death, heaven and hell—the big questions in life. Corporal Gilmetti had been shot in the jaw by an enemy sniper. He was Catholic, and the priest was there, too. The priest had already anointed and prayed with him. Then, without missing a beat, Gilmetti asked me a most unexpected question: "Chaplain, tell me, do girls like scars on a guy? Tell me they like them."

I laughed. He laughed. I smiled and said, "Absolutely. And yours will be just perfect. Noticeable enough but not too bad, and you'll have a pretty purple heart and a great story to go with them. The girls will go wild."

He laughed again and said, "Thanks, Chaplain, that's what I needed to know." We continued to talk about his family and his life back home. We talked about his hopes and dreams and we talked about how lucky he was.

I did not often carry my camera; the places where I worked—the hospital and Personnel Retrieval and Processing—had for obvious reasons strict rules regulating photography. But I was lucky that day, too. The day Corporal Gilmetti came through I had my camera. After we talked and right before he left, I asked, "Can I take your picture? You can say no if you're not comfortable."

He was silent for a moment, obviously weighing the option. None of us like our picture taken when we are not looking our best. He thought about it for awhile and finally said, "Sure, why not? It's not every day you're shot and live to tell about it. Yeah, go ahead. Just promise to send me a copy." So I snapped the picture and we exchanged emails.

There were others of the many patients we treated who were combat wounded and who, like Corporal Gilmetti, were able to interact with us as we were working on them. I probably prayed with and for all these guys, maybe even read some Scripture. I don't remember. That wasn't the important part of the story for them or for me. Each had been in the fight not even an hour before arriving on our doorstep. For them, it was more important that I listen and sit in awe of their stories and their wisdom as they recognized and experienced the reality of war up close and personally, now bearing its visible wounds on their bodies. The power was in the presence of one another. Somehow perfunctory prayer and Scripture reading offered in a traditional way would have tainted the sacred and powerful moment of warriors fresh off the battlefield.

✦ ✦ ✦

The corpsmen worked to start the IV line. The Marine talked and even laughed a little. From initial appearances, that was a good sign. Then, however, the doctor said something that didn't sound so good; even for the untrained the comment seemed ominous. He said, "In a little while, when we're done working on you here and before we move you for your trip to Balad, I am going to have to put a breathing tube down your throat." Obviously the situation was serious. He also explained to the young Marine lying motionless on the ER table, "But right now we are going to have to put a catheter in your penis to drain the urine."

The young Marine protested, saying, "Man, come on, no way. You don't have to do that, do you?"

"Yeah, we really do."

"Well, okay," the Marine begrudgingly agreed, knowing he really didn't have a choice but adding for good measure, "as long as you don't jam anything up my ass." Well, in this business there are no guarantees, and what he didn't know is that each patient actually does get that kind of check for internal intestinal bleeding. He'd already had his. But we all laughed and marveled at his sense of humor in the midst of what was obviously a serious injury.

It's funny how one's perspective changes. Not more than two weeks prior it was wrenching as I watched at the bedside of a patient, speaking softly into his ear while he writhed and screamed as they tried to get a catheter placed. Now, by contrast, the silence was wrenching. How I wanted to see that same writhing and screaming reaction today! We all did. In a place dedicated to alleviating suffering, paradoxically we wanted this young man to feel pain. Feeling, any feeling; reaction, any reaction would have been cause for celebration. Shot in the neck by a sniper, barring a miracle, this handsome, fit young man was destined to be a quadriplegic. He lay unmoving and unfeeling as every appendage of his body was poked and prodded. *Damn, he was the second one today shot in the neck! There was a sniper out there and he was good.* There was no hope for the first guy. We worked on him for awhile but he was dead; a gaping hole in the neck had severed the spinal cord—more than severed, really: it had blown a whole chunk out. Some would say the Marine now in front of us was the lucky one;

he was still alive. Who knows? It was too early to make a judgment like that, and only he would be able to make that determination. I'm sure there would be many days in the future when he would wonder. Although he was talkative and had a great sense of humor, I think he was in shock, both physical and psychic.

He talked about a lot of things. He talked about his mama back home. As he talked about her I thought about how her life would forever be changed. Just as her son was launching into adult life, chances are high he would now forever live with her at home . . . if he lived at all. There had been patients who were totally alert and talkative, just like this one, who later during surgery went to sleep and never woke up. That was part of the concern with this guy, as his wound was on the spinal cord, close to the nerves that control breathing. So there was a real possibility that once intubated he might stay that way. He talked about his car and his girlfriends. Outwardly we smiled but inwardly we were sad because without a miracle, he would never drive a car again and might never have another girlfriend. I was hopeful for him, though, because I knew that the love of his mother and his attitude full of humor and strength would help him in the difficult days ahead.

He got hit and ultimately was out of the fight. He was on his way home, but now he would fight an even more difficult battle every day. Every day into the foreseeable future, long after the troops eventually come home and long after the Iraq war fades into American history, this Marine will still be in the fight of his life. We were looking at one of the many, many thousands of seriously wounded veterans who in previous wars would never have survived. In many ways the sight of this young Marine was more gut-wrenching and heartbreaking than seeing the dead. As he bantered back and forth about sticking things in his penis and his butt, I knew he didn't know or was not allowing himself to hear the reality of his situation as the doctors worked on him and talked. But all of us around the stretcher knew. We shot each other knowing looks. Yes, a reaction as they jammed the catheter in would have made my morning. I prayed for physical pain that morning. My prayer was not answered.

ROUND AND ROUND IT GOES

Round and round the Ferris wheel circled. The movement was mesmerizing. Its bright lights were a sharp contrast to the darkness all around. It was nearly midnight, but judging from the lights there was still plenty of action at the amusement park. I thought about families enjoying their time together. I had gone to Disneyland with my kids just before I left for Iraq, and they'd promised to take me back there when I got home. This was no Disneyland. It was a small park in a small town, but still there were probably kids laughing and squealing in delight. I wondered whether there was cotton candy. The rest of the town looked sleepy and calm in contrast.

It could have been a small town anywhere. I couldn't help but stare at the sight: How normal, but how peculiar! This was Ramadi, the very heart of Iraq's Al Anbar province. There had been a lot of action here for at least two or three years, and by all accounts it was still happening. The region had an interesting distinction. For awhile it was home to the most dangerous road on the planet. It was the place where the Explosive Ordnance Disposal guys were busy every day. It was the place where other units were kept busy outside the wire, too. And yet here in the middle of the abnormal was the normal; in the middle of war was the hint at peace. The paradox was striking. It was confusing. My head was spinning anyway, and this made it spin in rhythm with the Ferris wheel. I knew it was impossible, but for a second I wondered whether I could visit that little park. I wanted to ride the Ferris wheel.

The helicopter landed briefly and we waited. We took off again for a short hop to the landing area at the base. I watched the lights from the Ferris wheel grow smaller and disappear, but I never forgot the sight.

Months after I got home from Iraq, I was at a gas station near my house. A guy stood at the pump next to me. I noticed his haircut. I noticed his shirt. Our shirts matched—well, sort of. I was wearing my favorite Ramadi sweatshirt. He was wearing a Ramadi shirt, too. And so I took a chance: "Were you in Ramadi?"

He looked up and said, "Yes, just got back a few weeks ago."

It doesn't take long to pump a tank of gas and there were so many things I wanted to say to him in a short time. Somehow I think I managed, with chaplain-like caring, to say, "Welcome home" and ask in a general way, "How was it for you over there?" But what I really wanted to know about was the Ferris wheel, and so I asked. "Is the amusement park with the Ferris wheel still there? I will never forget flying into Ramadi after midnight and seeing it lit up and going round and round and round."

He gave me an interesting look. I don't know whether up until then he didn't believe that I'd been in Iraq, but his face lit up the lights in the amusement park as he told me a little about his time there. Then he shook his head sadly and said, "I know where you're talking about. No, we had to shut that down. It was being used by the bad guys. It was too dangerous for us and the town."

I nodded my understanding. "Too bad; well, when they open it up again we will know things are getting better in Iraq. Maybe someday I'll get to go back and actually ride that Ferris wheel."

He gave me a funny look and said, "Well, maybe, but no thanks, not me; I've had enough of Ramadi. That was my second time there."

I agreed with him. "Yeah, I hope you don't have to go again." We said our good-byes and were lost in remembering the lights of Ramadi.

JUST ANOTHER NIGHT

LAST NIGHT AN ENEMY PRISONER OF WAR, or perhaps the more politically acceptable term, a detainee, slept crumpled in Bed 6, twisted and contorted in the blankets he'd brought with him. He never looked comfortable. Presumably he lay asleep, but who knows whether he was able to rest. No doubt the problem was more than physical discomfort; there was probably a lot on his mind, too.

Tonight a young Marine in his early twenties was in Bed 6. He was not so much crumpled in body as he was crumpled in spirit. He lay there trying to sleep but couldn't; without a doubt he had too much on his mind as well.

Next to him in Bed 7 lay his buddy, who only two months ago had occupied Bed 6. Then it was a gunshot wound to the legs; today it was an improvised explosive device blast. Their physical wounds were in many ways superficial. They would heal quickly. The other wounds, however, were very deep. I'm not sure they will ever really heal. Does one ever heal from blacking out in a blast only to wake up and find his friend's head lying in his lap? Although apparently the friend still had a slight pulse at the scene, he was mortally wounded. Both legs were blown off. He bled out. I guess one consolation for those of us thinking about it tonight, and what might bring his buddies some consolation later, is that the guy probably never knew what hit him. He probably blacked out like the rest of them and then mercifully never regained consciousness.

Nick and his friend were shocked, still in disbelief. They were so close to their destination, not more than two miles away, and hit on their commute home. They'd spent Friday at Al Taqqadum resting, relaxing, having a meal in the chow hall and using the Internet café. They were on their way back to their combat outpost for another routine work week. The vehicle commander shook his head and talked a little. There wasn't much talk, though. There was nothing any of us could say and there was certainly nothing any of us could do to make the situation better, so mostly we sat together in silence. Nick and his buddy cried together and held each other and waited for their other buddy to come out of surgery. They were four young guys riding together in a vehicle after a night out on the town. Now one is gone. Only three remain. That's the way it happens here; one or two are taken out.

THAT SMELL WAS ALWAYS THERE WITH BLAST CASUALTIES, THE HORRIBLE, UNMISTAKABLE SMELL OF BURNED FLESH.

There seldom are large numbers killed at once. These are the faces of the all-volunteer force. These are the faces of fellow reservists from the heartland of America who have other lives, real lives outside the military. They serve willingly and well, but especially on a night like tonight they wonder why.

In an odd way it was strangely similar to accidents back home. Kids and young adults, or really anybody for that matter, ride together in a vehicle and a terrible accident occurs. Some live and some die, who knows who and who knows why. I could tell that the vehicle commander, although right in front in me, was really still back there at the scene; his voice trailed off as he relived the event. "I usually ride in that seat. I don't know why I wasn't in that seat today. Joseph wasn't even supposed to be with our unit out here, but he knew some of the guys and asked to deploy with us. These guys were all there for me when I got shot and was lying in that field. They wrapped my legs and kept me laughing. But there was nothing I could do for them tonight." This young Marine had just made sergeant and was taking his responsibility seriously. He was the senior man in the Humvee and now one of his guys was dead, one of his friends, one of his brothers. Trying to explain the depth of his loss, he said, "We all may have different mothers but we are all brothers."

I thought back to Joseph lying crumpled in the body bag. He was turned to one side, his bloody arm and hand above his head. He looked fine on top. There was just a little hint of blood, and his uniform still looked remarkably presentable. You could read "US Marines" on the left side and his name tape on the right. Looking further, however, the telltale signs of the trauma were readily apparent. Both legs were gone above the knees; there was no mystery as to how or why he died. I was surprised there were not visible burns, because there was an awful odor lingering in the air. That smell was always there with blast casualties, the horrible, unmistakable smell of burned flesh. There was nothing more we could do for him except send him home. He was zipped in a black body bag and the bag was draped with an American flag. The hospital staff gathered and prayed for him and his family and his buddies back home. We manned the rails (honoring the dead by standing at attention on both sides of the passageway) as he was taken from the hospital by Personnel Retrieval and Processing. We said good-bye to a young Marine named Joseph and got back to work taking care of his three buddies, a couple of Army guys, and a conglomeration of Iraqi patients. Just another evening at the hospital in TQ.

THE DAD, THE BOY, AND THE STUFFED DOG

L ITTLE BROWN HANDS CLUTCHED the little brown stuffed dog. It was not so different from the stuffed animal I slept with every night while I was growing up. I was about three years old when I named my stuffed dog "Bow" (as in "bow-wow"). I wondered what this Iraqi boy called his fake furry friend. It was nice; the stuffed animal seemed to bring him comfort. He was after all in an uncomfortable place: in a hospital ward with his head bandaged such that his eyes were wrapped, too. The scene was a study in contrasts and paradoxes, but then again, this whole place was. The boy was quickly leaving childhood behind. He was almost a teenager at age twelve. More than that he lived in a war zone, and war ages you beyond your years. Yet somehow tonight he seemed younger, more vulnerable than a boy about to become a man. Maybe it was the stuffed dog.

The boy looked as comfortable as one could be under the circumstances, leaned casually against a large blue vinyl prop pillow in a position one might seek to lounge and watch TV or enjoy a leisurely breakfast in bed. He was not, however, lounging by choice, nor did it seem that there would be breakfast in bed. Instead, the nightstand, which really was a small green folding table, offered a midnight snack of green Gatorade and a blueberry muffin wrapped in plastic. Somehow I doubted whether he knew it was there, and even if he did know, he would be hard pressed to actually consume it. The IV line hung from a cord above his bed and ran into his left arm. He looked as comfortable and as peaceful as he could, a little calmer than earlier, when he was crying. Nobody knew exactly how he'd been injured. He had some sort of puncture wound to the abdomen. Luckily for him it was probably nothing very serious.

The kid's black t-shirt matched the jet-black eyes of his newfound stuffed dog friend. The white letters on the shirt matched the white gauze bandage wrapped around his head, and the maroon trim around the neck of the shirt accentuated the red in his lips.

An Iraqi man lay in the bed next to him. He didn't look nearly as comfortable as the boy did. Turned 180 degrees from normal, he was all scrunched up with his head jammed against the metal footboard, covered with the blankets he'd brought with him. The blankets were brown with charcoal-gray strips of fabric sewn across for decoration. He also had a blanket that was softer in texture and lighter in color, almost an ivory. His shoes sat neatly at mid-span under the bed. They were black, but it was hard to tell because

IT WASN'T ME, I'M JUST AN INNOCENT BYSTANDER!

they were covered with a fine layer of brown mud. The brown mud color coordinated well with the brown blanket. It had rained hard here early in the week and there were still puddles all over. The ground here does not absorb the water. His nice black shoes decorated with little buckles were a mess, and so was he. Like the boy, he had his head bandaged and eyes wrapped. His gray hair made him look older than he probably was; war has a way of wearing on you.

Both patients, presumably father and son, were treated and awaiting transportation. The nurse was attentive—more attentive than one would expect given the mildness of the injuries. The corpsman was as well. He sat at the foot of the bed in an old cushioned desk chair watching and waiting, his M-16 at the ready. A Marine, one assigned to hospital security, was close by, too. They had to be. The patients were detainees suspected of planting or getting ready to plant an improvised explosive device. Digging holes—especially around roadways—is not a wise thing to do here. It can well lead to holes of another kind, the kind that go through and through a body. This kid was lucky. Whatever may have caused his puncture wound, it was not a gunshot.

The scene was surreal. This boy, who was not even a teenager and perhaps not old enough to make his own decisions, now lay wounded and weeping, clutching a stuffed animal. Only a few hours earlier he was caught while participating—willingly or unwillingly, wittingly or unwittingly—against us. He and his dad now were held captive with us for a few hours, waiting to be transported to a prison. It was a sad situation. We saw almost daily the results of IEDs, the massive explosive trauma to the human body. Some lived, some died, and some who did live will probably wish they had died. But the situation didn't represent something as simple as "us against them," "good guy/bad guy" mentality, and we knew that. We had talked enough with guys assigned to the reconstruction teams who brought the wounded into the hospital to know that a lot of Iraqis felt they were in a no-win situation.

We looked at the father and son lying in the two beds and wondered. Were they really against us, or were they simply faced with a situation no one should ever have to endure? Their country is in shambles. The economy is struggling. Life is not normal. People wonder and worry day to day how to feed their families. "Bad" guys interact with "average" Iraqis and either force or coerce them with threats or acts of violence or bribe them with money. We wondered out loud who could resist the temptation of planting bombs given an immediate threat to one's family or given the opportunity make money to feed that family for the next month. Would very many of us resist the immediate rewards for the promise of a better tomorrow someday in the future? In a war zone, future has little meaning. The immediate and present reality demands attention. For many, tomorrow may never come.

It was a sad situation, father and son captive and wounded. Could they be persuaded to work with us instead of against us? We knew there were probably a lot of people like that outside the wire, ones caught in the middle, caught in the crossfire, making decisions that sadly could cost American lives. Day after day our guys outside the wire work diligently to sort out friend and foe in a situation where you can't tell by looking. Our guys work hard to connect with and work with the local Iraqis seeking to rebuild their lives and their country. This man and his son were symbolic of so much. There was so much to think about, and it was complex. There are no easy answers. We sat quietly talking, keeping each other company in the early morning hours on the hospital ward. I guess we were trying to make sense of it, too. We'd probably been sitting and talking for at least an hour.

Then, just as the conversation was getting a little too serious, someone noticed the writing on the boy's shirt. When patients come into the hospital, often the clothes they arrive in are no longer usable, and so before leaving we provide them with clean clothing donated and sent to us by Americans back home. Such was the case with these guys. The nurse and corpsman had randomly grabbed clothing from the bag and dressed them, but no one up until this point had read the shirt or realized the irony.

It was all strange, but nothing stranger than the boy's shirt that summarized it all. *"It wasn't me, I'm just an innocent bystander!"* We all stared in disbelief. We longed to be able to take a picture. We didn't want to be part of a new prisoner photo scandal! The universe played a joke on us that night and we all appreciated it. We marveled. We wondered. We knew in that moment it was no "accident." It seemed strangely spiritual, almost like a Zen koan.

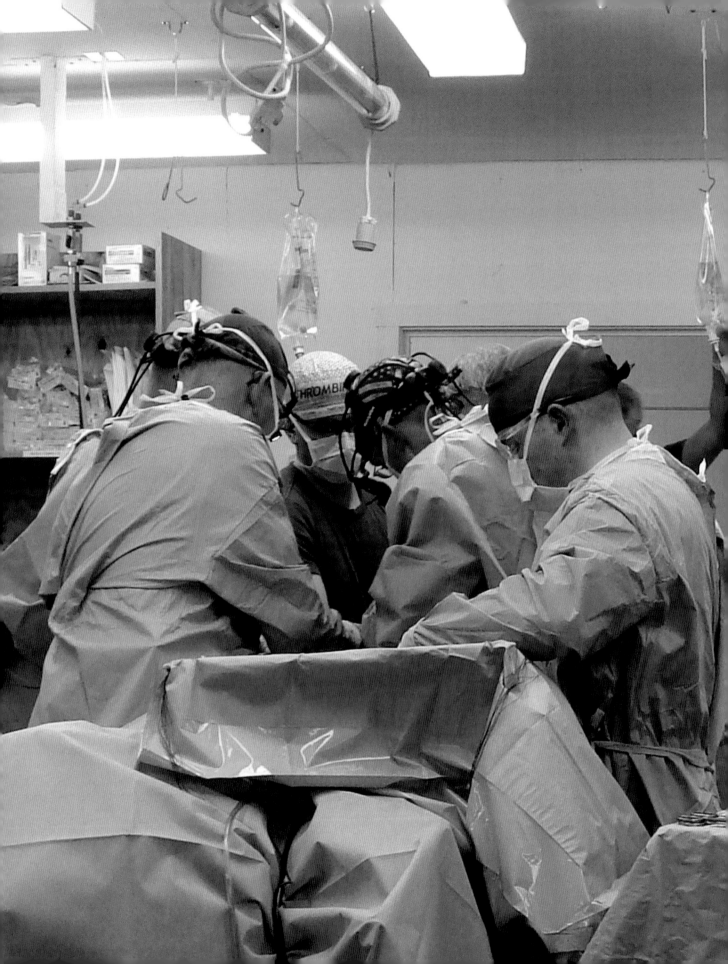

THE
GUNNY

THE FIRST PATIENT WAS OBVIOUS. The corpsmen and his unit members worked to extricate him from the rescue vehicle. He was a big guy and the litter was not cooperating. They were wrestling with it in the back of a seven-ton truck. Nonetheless, the scene was a welcome sight. At least the injured were at the hospital and not simply bodies delivered to the morgue. The Marine Corps green truck was also a welcome change from the desert-sand brown. And this extrication was easy compared to the one that had taken place within the hour just ten clicks away. The good news was that the sergeant was now here and able to get the best care possible. He had a chance to survive.

Three others, unfortunately, did not; two were removed from the Humvee before it burned but were unable to survive the devastating injuries. The remaining Marine was still stuck in the vehicle, and the vehicle was stuck where it was hit and still burning. His fate was obvious.

We were hopeful when the radio call first came in. It was for four urgent surgicals with head trauma, burns, and extremity damage. Sure, that's bad, but at least we were getting patients. But now battlefield reality hit us: we were getting only two patients, not four. Well, no time to think about that. Our attention turned to the patient in the ER. The sergeant was seriously burned but was still talking to the doctors and nurses as they began their work.

But where was the other patient? There were five people in the vehicle, and the revised call had been to stand by for two wounded. Yet no one else appeared from the back of the rescue vehicle.

Suddenly attention turned to the double doors of the ER. A Marine in a brown flight suit stained with soot and dust and a little blood walked in. He entered with a steady, determined stride. His gaze was steady and determined, too. A doctor met him halfway and they talked as they made their way toward one of the stations, a litter, in the ER.

His flak vest was still wrapped tightly around his upper body. The front was dirty but intact. The back of the vest gave clues to his recent close encounter. The heavy material covering the plates was shredded and stained with soot. Yet it was not only his vest; his face had a similar look. Pieces of skin were peeled back and hung in shreds, too. Soot, blood, and burns streaked his face. From head to toe the colors blended into an unusual blur of tan, browns, and charcoal black and gray.

In spite of how it looked, there was a lot of good news for this Marine. He'd walked in on his own power. His burns were bad but did not look terrible. He was still fully recognizable and did not have deep, serious, disfiguring burns. In fact, as he stood there in his stained flight suit and shredded flak vest and with his wounded face, he looked as if he'd come straight from wardrobe and makeup ready for a film shoot. He looked like a typecast John Wayne hero on a movie set. If this were a movie set, the role he would play would be senior noncommissioned officer, more affectionately known as the Gunny.

We had already been introduced to the Gunny, but little did we know that we were about to see him in an expanded role. He looked and played the part, but this was no act. We were seeing the real thing. The Gunny sported the shaved head and the customary tattoos that Marines are known for. He was large and well muscled, rugged and determined. We could hardly take our eyes off him. His presence and personal power was mesmerizing. But then the scene became even more intriguing. We looked up and his Marines, guys from his unit, had quietly slipped into the ER to watch. Technically they weren't supposed to be there, but no one in authority had the heart to kick them out. And quite frankly they didn't need to, because they were doing more good than harm. It was an amazing sight.

Six or eight of the Marines had spontaneously assembled themselves in two neat rows, an impromptu formation, behind the red line in the ER. Silently they stood the watch. They were there with their Gunny and he knew it. They watched every move; they watched the medical staff, and they watched the Gunny. They were worried. They were hopeful. In between procedures and tests and the requisite poking and prodding, the Gunny communicated with his guys from across the room. He smiled. He waved. He gave the thumbs-up sign. With each hopeful sign his guys relaxed. They were visibly relieved. They exchanged nods and smiles among themselves. They dared not speak; they didn't want to disrupt or take the chance of getting thrown out and relegated to the waiting room.

Although wounded and lying in the ER, via silent communication, command presence, unwavering focus, and calm demeanor, the Gunny led his men by example. Without a word, the older warrior taught the younger ones. I was transfixed. It might not have been a miracle, but it was awe-inspiring. I was privileged to witness Marine Corps leadership at its finest.

THAT WAS CLOSE

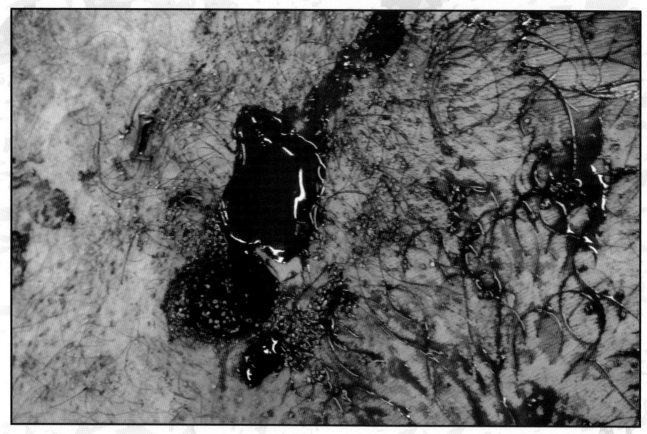

"I can't believe I got hit. I need to be out there with my guys helping them. They're young, inexperienced. I worry about them. Ya know when something happens like this, me gittin' shot, some of 'em just want to go shoot anything, anybody. They don't think. But that's dangerous. They gotta stop and think. I just hope they remember what I taught 'em and don't get crazy on me. I don't need to lose any of them like. . . ." His voice trailed off. He paused, became teary, and finished his thought more to himself than to me. Just above a whisper. "Like some of the guys I lost when I was here in 2004." Every now and then he'd wince in pain. He was shot near the hip and couldn't get comfortable.

I guess it's hard to lie down and feel relaxed with a bullet hole through the lower part of your body, where all the weight rests. I think the drugs helped a little. But beyond the physical pain, he was in emotional and spiritual pain. He even said as much. "Wow, I was okay, Chaplain, until you came up and said hello." It really wasn't that he wanted me to leave him alone but that my presence was a trigger, a trigger for stored grief from two and a half years ago, when he lost some of his guys. Perhaps it was also a trigger for many other current emotions: fear, anxiety, relief, and the realization of how close he'd just come to dying.

Some people are afraid of emotions. Many warriors think it's bad to feel, especially in the middle of a war zone. But feelings are real and powerful and part of what make us human. Recognized, managed, and integrated, they form important parts of our personal stories and memories and can motivate us in positive ways. The doctors, nurses, and corpsmen helped start him on the road to physical recovery. I'd like to think that by giving him permission and space to feel, I helped him begin the road to emotional and spiritual recovery. As happened so often at the bedside, we had a strangely private moment of shared emotion while surrounded by a lot a people and a lot of activity. The medics usually had patients for a very brief time—just long enough to stabilize them and release them back to their units or move them on for further care. That night was no different; it was just a short interaction. For the injured, my presence was somewhat like a valve on a pressure cooker, allowing him to let off a little steam in a short, intense burst.

THE BIG VOICE

IT WAS HALF PAST MIDNIGHT. I'd been in bed for about an hour, sleeping in the nude. When the only clothing choices are desert camouflage uniform or Marine Corps green PT gear, one's birthday suit seems like a nice alternative. *Boom! Boom! Boom*! Now I was awake. I thought, *wow that's closer than it's been before.* I asked myself a key question: *Was that incoming or outgoing?* Another key question followed: *Should I put clothes on?* I pondered the possibilities and ran the scenarios through my head. I was tired. I was sleepy. I was warm and cozy in my bed between my blue checkered Disney *Cars* movie sheets. I didn't want to get up, especially if it was not necessary. Yet I also imagined that if it was the real deal, I might have to evacuate quickly—or worse yet, maybe I'd be hit and they'd find me lying naked in my room. Oh, well, what difference would it make? Pretty much everyone who ends up going through medical ends up naked, so I'd be ready! *Boom, boom, boom*; the "cans" (our trailerlike rooms) rattled and shuddered with each volley. I had confidence in the Big Voice. I'd heard about the Big Voice. I knew it existed. I trusted it worked. I trusted it would warn me. I didn't hear the Big Voice, so I figured I was safe. I rolled over to go back to sleep, and the booming and the rattling and the shaking continued. I believed and assumed it was outgoing artillery fire—what a lovely, peaceful lullaby to lull me back to sleep!

The Big Voice: I'd heard about it but had never heard it, never experienced it in person. I knew someday I would. *"All clear, code green,"* the small hand-held radios blared. *Hmm*, that was related to the Big Voice. I found out later that the warning had actually gone off a few times, but I was busy in the hospital or asleep in my room. I tried not to think about the nagging little fact that had just become apparent—*Great, can't hear the warning where I work or where I sleep. Oh well, I guess what I don't know won't hurt me.* At least I wouldn't spend time or energy worrying about it, wasting time and energy on something I couldn't do anything about anyway. Maybe some of the areas weren't wired for sound; maybe it wasn't working right. There were no main speakers blaring, only the small ones on the radios attached to each belt. We looked at each other quizzically. We hadn't even known we were taking incoming. We were busy with patients, busy with a mass casualty; we would know soon enough if there were any other casualties associated with the recent indirect fire incident. It really was not our problem as long as it didn't hit the hospital. We didn't need to be casualties. The last thing we needed was a mass casualty times two, casualty upon casualty. It was always a possibility but, thankfully, seldom likely.

I REALIZED THE BIG VOICE IS A LOT LIKE THE WIZARD OF OZ, HELPFUL IF YOU BELIEVE. BUT THERE IS A NIGGLING UNSPOKEN REALITY.

85

Well, finally one day I heard the Big Voice. *"Incoming, incoming, incoming."* The speaker system in the the dining facility sounded the warning. Everyone continued eating and talking and laughing. People gave various renditions of what the Big Voice might say to make it funnier or more hip, such as, "Get down, get down, get down. They be shootin' at you," or simply, "Watch out, they be blastin' your ass." But now and into the foreseeable future, I'm sure it will remain an irritatingly loud warning blast with a grating humanlike voice that follows, screaming, "Incoming, incoming, incoming."

There was nothing else to do but continue laughing, talking, and eating, and that's okay. We were in one of the safer places on base. Theoretically the roof structure is hardened to withstand a blast. The standard instruction is to seek cover and stand fast for fifteen minutes after the warning sounds. It was obvious that some people ignored the warning and walked out of the building, intent on getting on with their day. But for many, me included, it provided an excuse for dessert. Heck, if we're about to get blown up, we might as well live it up. We had time to kill, so why not? Besides, if we were to be hit or die, how better to do it than laughing and talking and eating with friends?

Anticipation is often more difficult and arduous than the real thing, and at least for that day it held true. I'd had another first, another initiation in the war zone. I'd had my first experience with the Big Voice. Funny, the Big Voice wasn't nearly as big or scary as I'd expected. Of course, that's easy to say when the incoming is nowhere near where you are. I know it would have been more thrilling if it had been close: if you could hear it, see it, or feel it. It's pretty safe at Al Taqqadum, but nothing ever is 100 percent, and we were, after all, in a war zone. A month or two before I got there, a mortar or rocket was lobbed in and hit close to the dining facility. The blast and the fragments were contained in sand berms and barriers. It was around noon. People walking to and from lunch saw, felt, and heard the blast, and hearts beat just a little faster. TQ was lucky that day.

I realized the Big Voice is a lot like the Wizard of Oz, helpful to a point and helpful if you believe. But there is a niggling unspoken reality. The Big Voice is good but by the time you hear it, somewhere or something on base has already been hit. By contrast, every time the artillery fires an outgoing volley there is an odd comfort. And so the reality of war creates a dilemma for me. I listen and hope for outgoing artillery fire. I listen with mixed or not-so-mixed feelings, knowing it is an important part of defending me against indirect fire lobbed at the base. But I know, too, that each time, something or someone else is being destroyed.

There was a strange beauty to the old mortars and mines from another war now cast aside. In this setting they bring color and texture to an otherwise barren landscape, a much better use than their originally-intended purpose.

SLOW DANCING

IT WAS LATE DECEMBER. The dance of the sugarplum fairies was sure to be playing somewhere this time of year . . . but not here, at least not now, probably not ever. Instead we watched a live performance of another kind, a dance to another beat.

It was early morning as we waited at the edge of the runway in Al Taqqadum on the way to Fallujah. It was dark and desolate except for the lights scattered across the runway: red, white, and blue. They were the only lights allowed here, but they were colorful and festive. They felt strangely patriotic. Each light marked part of a specific pattern—a taxi way, a work or waiting area. Marines worked around the airstrip moving pallets of mail, remnants of Christmas mail now sure to be late. The sky was pitch black. It was very dark. It was desolate, too—desolate except for the people waiting for flights and those coordinating them. We stood in the darkness and looked out toward the few lights. Each of us silently hoped the darkness would cover us. TQ was still hit periodically and many of the hits fell near the runways;

most fell harmlessly, but all it would take is a lucky shot. Yes, the darkness enveloped us, and that was a good thing.

Behind our waiting/staging area was a group of port-a-johns. The port-a-johns were surrounded by large concrete blast barriers. It was good that at least there was a little security! What could be worse than taking a direct hit while using a port-a-john? That area was unlit as well. There were no trail markers, no lights of any kind. One was left using small colored flashlights (usually pinpoint red, green, or blue), or we simply tried to find our way in the dark by feel.

> I WAS NOT WATCHING A PERFORMANCE OF *THE NUTCRACKER,* BUT I FELT LUCKY. NOT MANY PEOPLE HAVE EVER WITNESSED WHAT WE JUST DID.

Creature comforts were nonexistent in this boarding area. There were very few choices. You could stand or you could sit on the ground. There was a third alternative chosen by a few: some lay down on their packs and tried to sleep. Most chose to stand. Some talked; some smoked; some were lost in their own thoughts.

We were all loosely formed up on the chem light trail, dutifully waiting where we'd been told. We were tired. It was late, well past midnight. We'd worked all day and we were still working. The days and nights run together here. We were in TQ on our way to Fallujah, each with our own task or mission. No one moved around the area of operations just for fun or just because. It wasn't like at home, where you decide to visit the neighboring town and just go. It wasn't so simple here. I knew where these other people were going but I wondered why. What were their missions? Someone deemed it important enough to give permission and schedule them on flights. Flights were a commodity here but not necessarily easy to get. What were they facing the next day? It was only a few days before Christmas. Were they going "home" to Fallujah for Christmas? My schedule was set for me to be "home" (at TQ) for Christmas. Would I make it?

I was looking forward to seeing Fallujah. I'd heard so many stories from the Marines at Kaneohe Bay during the summer of 2005. They had been in the battle for Fallujah. I had seen those places in my mind as they described the experience. Now at least I would get close—not in the city, but on the base.

It was relatively quiet for a time. A few people talked, and a forklift and a truck did their own private dance. But we hoped it would get noisy soon. We were tired of waiting, though no one complained. There was no point. Then in the distance we heard the welcome sound: thump, thump, thump. It began to get louder. Barely visible through the darkness of the moonless desert, where the blackness of the sky and the blackness of the sand meet at the horizon and form an unending expanse, the Cobras appeared. Commanding and powerful, ever watchful, they effortlessly penetrated the darkness. The 53s landed some distance away and began a slow taxi.

I was fascinated. I listened. I watched. I felt. They were dancing in the distance to the steady beat of their own rhythm. In time, in step, carefully choreographed and moving together, one led, one followed. They were big, lumbering helicopters but there was a grace about them. Were these ours? Yes, I thought so. But we wouldn't know for sure for awhile. Slowly, slowly they moved. Our perception was distorted by the darkness. Two 46s joined the dance. They landed behind the others and just stayed put, almost like backup dancers supporting the stars. They added to the rhythm and added to the steady beat. The 46s seemed content to let the 53s lead. The 53s twirled; they moved; they paused. They moved again at a steady pace. They turned the corner, moved forward, and then turned again. They passed us. Were they teasing us with their enticing dance? Meanwhile we stood fast. Were we the audience or part of the supporting cast? We were on the sidelines, watching the shadowy figures dance in the darkness.

Finally it was our turn to move. We chased the dancers. They had gone a long way past our staging area. We were walking fast. It was almost a jog across the uneven dark ground. Desert rocks and sand made progress hard, but the dancers encouraged us. They called to us to join them. The steady whir of their rotors made music. We juggled backpacks and gear. We wore Kevlar and flak. Our movement, our dance, was not the most graceful. We followed our leader, the one person authorized to have a light on now. In darkness our single-file line moved ever closer.

Our boarding passes were ready. The "passes" were literally on our hands. Everyone had 406CF (the ASR number and destination code) written in felt marker. It was our ticket to ride. Each of us was carefully checked and double-checked. Getting on the wrong flight here would be a problem.

Ear plugs muffled some of the noise, but the steady rotor beat pulsated and penetrated your body, your mind, your soul. The desert night wind blew cold. The blast from the engine blew hot exhaust fumes. Hot and cold air mixed together. The rotors flicked and teased the air, lifting, moving, inviting one to enter further into the dance. Like a strong, vibrant dancer wanting to lift and entwine his partner moving in unison, moving as one, yes, we were invited in. Entering in through the warm exhaust air felt good on the chilly winter night. I thought about summer in Iraq and knew it wouldn't be so inviting or charming then. I felt lucky to be there now and not then. Aboard and seated, we settled in.

We lifted off, and I was kind of sad. The performance was over. The strange stage and the unique dance, the unusual lights, costumes, beats and rhythms, and dancers moving in carefully practiced choreography were finished. It was late December in Iraq. I was not watching a performance of *The Nutcracker* in a lovely theater somewhere, but I felt lucky. Not many people have ever witnessed what we just did. We were part of a special performance. Flight and ground crews work nightly there with practiced skill. Regularly scheduled and emergency flights move people, here, there and all around. Sometimes we watch and are a part of the dance; other nights we just listen as the steady rhythm lulls us to sleep like a familiar lullaby. Night after night, the helicopters dance.

REMEMBERING
LUKE

"I GOT BACK FROM IRAQ IN FEBRUARY," I SAID.

The HM1 (corpsman) responded. "Really? I got back in March."

Curious, I asked, "Who were you over there with?"

He said, "Same unit I'm with now, Third Anglico. We were in Ramadi."

I looked more closely at the guy sitting across from me and asked a question. I already sensed the answer. "You were in the EOD compound at Ramadi?"

He answered, "Yes, Ma'am, right there."

My mind drifted back to the scenes of Ramadi as I told him what he already knew as well: "I was there too, in fact exactly a year ago. Just last night I was rereading my journal entry about Ramadi and reliving my four days spent with the Explosive Ordnance Disposal guys. I wish I were back there."

"Yes, Ma'am, I was right there too," he said. "Right there with Crash, Fire and Rescue and Combat Stress and EOD. I thought you looked familiar. I remember when you came to visit."

We continued to talk and laugh and remember Ramadi. It was fun to reconnect with someone I'd met in passing while "over there." Now I understand the immediate camaraderie combat veterans have even long after a war. I know the scene will repeat again and again in the years to come, whenever I meet someone who was in Iraq. There is a special bond that is forged only by going to war together.

MANY PEOPLE I WAS THERE WITH DIDN'T AGREE WITH THIS WAR. LUKE WAS ONE OF THOSE PEOPLE.

Not only were the corpsman and I there at the same time but we knew the same people. Curiosity again got me and I asked, "Hey what happened after I left Iraq? I tried to stay until all my guys came home but they made me leave with Headquarters' Company. I heard a couple guys got killed." It was such a small compound that I knew I was sure to have seen them, maybe even talked to them.

He paused and looked at me for a moment before he answered. "Yeah, you didn't know? EOD lost a couple guys: a corpsman and a staff sergeant. It must have happened right after you left Iraq."

I was stunned. My heart sank. It was hard to lose anybody, but these guys weren't just anybody. They weren't just American names on a list of casualties. These were my guys from one of my units. I knew them. We had talked and laughed, smoked and joked around the warm campfire on a couple of crisp, cool late fall Ramadi nights. I'd watched them come and go on missions, usually late at night or in the early morning hours. They'd even invited me to ride along, a doable feat in theory but not a likely event or justifiable risk for the chaplain in reality. We'd talked about a few of their close calls, about reality and the grim possibilities. But we talked, too, about training and about mental toughness. These guys chose this profession and are good at what they do. They were ever mindful of the risks but were motivated by internal rewards inexplicable to those on the outside. I was honored to be let into their world, if only for a brief moment. And so now I needed to know, and I asked the inevitable question: "Who?"

He responded bluntly, "The corpsman was HN Emch and the staff sergeant was Gould."

I was stunned and sat in shock as the news soaked in. Yes, I knew these guys; they were my guys, and exactly one year after I'd visited Ramadi, while at home at my reserve center, I found out they died. My mind spun with images. I tried to remember their faces. I had pictures of some of the guys in Ramadi. I wondered whether I had theirs. I thought of the dusty little base at Ramadi and the little compound where the vehicles were parked neatly in a row in front of the old single-story buildings that had once housed Saddam's military. Now our guys lived and worked there. Road-clearing missions began and ended there. One of the vehicles, the Cougar, was so reliable and so trusted, battle hardened and tested. There had never been a serious loss with one of those; everyone felt more confident riding in that vehicle. That's what I would have ridden in had I been able to do so. My mind spun with images of improvised explosive devices, and unfortunately it spun, too, with images of what the after-effects of the blast must have looked like. I'd seen my share and knew all too well.

The corpsman did a good job at explaining the details as he knew and remembered them. I was glad to know.

"The guys got blown up loading an IED into the Cougar. Thankfully it was instantaneous; they probably never knew they'd been hit." His voice trailed off and stopped. He was obviously remembering that day when he heard the news. We were lost in our own thoughts, but together we remembered Ramadi. He continued, "Yeah, it was hard on everybody; you know it was such a small compound. We knew each other pretty well. It was hard, too, because those guys were due to go home. One was leaving in a day or so and the other in a couple weeks." Neither of us gave voice to the obvious feeling and sort of unwritten rule that death is more unfair, more unacceptable, so close to someone's scheduled return date. We knew the families believed the worst was over and were just counting down the final few days. It's too painful to contemplate how close they were to being finished or to think of the homecoming and party plans.

✦ ✦ ✦

When I'd returned home in February, for the first time in months I watched TV and listened to the radio. I was angry. I wanted news about Iraq: comprehensive news about Ramadi, Fallujah, and my guys both American and Iraqi. I thought of the people still there. I would never know what happened to most of them. There was very little news. Instead, I got repetitive broadcasts about various stars getting into or out of trouble. The exploits of Anna Nicole Smith or Britney Spears or a long list of others don't matter to me and don't make a difference in my life or the world. Why is that considered news? I was angry then and, as I sit here today, I'm angry now. My EOD guys, their two lives and those of many others like them, are given in sacrifice yet they don't make the headlines at all.

"How are you today?" the doctor asked, expecting an obviously normal "fine, thank you" response. I was there to fulfill a simple annual reserve medical-check requirement. I just stared at him without saying a word. He stared back at me, still waiting for my answer.

I shook my head to literally and symbolically shake myself out of a daze and said, "Oh, sorry. I'm a little stunned actually. I just found out from HM1 that one of the EOD guys and one of the corpsmen I knew in Iraq were killed shortly after I left. I didn't know until just now."

The young doctor, at least young in the Navy as evidenced by the lone ribbon on his chest, now was the one who gave me a momentary blank look. It was my turn to stare at him and wait for his reply. Finally he responded with, "Wow." He quickly busied himself with the task at hand.

We finished my health assessment and I ended the conversation with a question and a statement, "Will you be going to Iraq? I hope you do; it's an awesome experience."

The doctor gave me another dumbfounded stare, and by the look on his face I don't think I won a convert. He gave me a weak smile, shook his head, and said, "No I don't think so."

The HM1 and I met up later that day to look at my Ramadi pictures. The young man in the photograph smiled at us from the computer screen. HM1 said, "Yep, that's Emch. That's a great picture of him." We smiled sad smiles in return. Who knows exactly why I snapped the shot? There were many photo opportunities I never took. This one I did. It really is just a snapshot of a guy sitting on a simple wooden bench leaning against a neutral-colored wall. Yet there is a spiritual quality that comes through. The picture feels like a casual portrait that captured the essence of the place and the personality of the young man. His wry smile hinted at his underlying sense of humor. His blue sandals matched the blue smoke-pit bucket and were a stark contrast to the desert-sand brown of the nomex flight suit. It is an elegantly simple photo but it speaks volumes, especially now that Luke can no longer speak for himself. It captured a moment in Ramadi time.

The contrasting blue flip-flop sandals and the casual, relaxed look and smile drew my attention. I wanted to remember the EOD corpsmen. These are bright young men with lots to offer and a world ahead of them. They choose willingly to serve with the Marines and then they choose an even more difficult, more dangerous, and greater task than most. They serve as medical support with EOD. They take turns riding on the teams to dismantle and recover IEDs or roadside bombs. They help keep the roadways clear and ultimately bring greater security and stability to the area. Ramadi was an active area in late 2006 and early 2007. Everyone knew without saying a word that every mission was serious, potentially deadly. There was really nothing to talk about; that's just the way it was.

From a logical perspective, the loss is such a waste. Some of our best and brightest of the all-volunteer force get killed. Many of us, like HN Luke Emch, have (or had) other options in life. We did not have to join the military and we didn't have to serve with the Marines in a combat zone. But we did. Luke did. Some would ask the question, "And what is the reward?" They would in turn cynically answer, "A futile death in the desert." But those of us who have been there know the reward is deep and intangible, some might even say spiritual. It is an inner knowing that you answered a call to serve, to serve a purpose greater than oneself, to be part of a team trying to make a difference. But it is even simpler than that. It is to serve not a grand or glorious cause but to serve the people closest to you: the guy on your right and the guy on your left. It sounds so trite and so cliché, but in the day-to-day reality of a war zone, it is nothing more than that.

One may not agree with the bigger national policies or blunt techniques of our international persuasion, but corpsmen like doctors, nurses, and chaplains volunteer to serve the human needs of both friend and foe in a combat zone. In fact, many people I was there with didn't agree with this war. Luke was one of those people. By his own admission he was a "raging liberal." Yet he was there because he loved his country. He was also by his own admission patriotic. He felt a duty to serve in the military and never understood why more people didn't have the same impulse. He was an interesting study in contrasts, and many people did not understand how he could hold both views so vigorously.

All of us realized the absurdity of spending too much time thinking about or discussing the politics and advisability of our current involvement in Iraq. That was truly futile. It didn't matter. We were already there in the middle of it. Wishing it were not so or thinking it should be different was not going to change the situation. We had no control over the big picture. We could philosophize all we wanted, but at the beginning of a mission or at the end of a difficult day, what good would that have done except to make your head hurt or to make you angry at the people or systems (whoever and whatever you personally believe those to be) that make war necessary in the first place?

We talked about the war enough to know we were tired of seeing dead bodies. We talked about it enough to know we had serious questions about Iraq. But we knew it best to reserve those conversations for another time and place, maybe at a coffeehouse in a college town back home before the next presidential election. Unfortunately, some of the best and brightest such as Luke will not be there; Luke will be unable to add his unique mixture of battle-hardened savvy and his liberal leanings to the conversations. Perhaps, however, if we listen carefully we might hear some of his words of wisdom. I hope so.

OPPORTUNITY KNOCKS

Quaint lakeside desert community holds many opportunities for year-round residents. A place with a friendly multi-cultural flavor has a charm of yester-year within minutes of local town and within easy driving distance to capital city. Enjoy spectacular romantic sunset views over the lake and the unspoiled dark night-time skies filled with stars. This is desert living at its finest. TQ is a master-planned community so everything is within easy walking distance. If you've been looking for a place to call home, look no further. You've found the place to belong: a place to live, a place to work, a place to play. Act quickly, opportunities are limited and openings that become available usually fill fast. Don't be left out. Call today for more information about this desert oasis.

Opportunity knocks. Redevelopment district specials. Some lots have spectacular water views of Lake Habbaniyah, others are in town, within walking distance to churches, restaurants, shopping, and the entertainment district. Some are move in ready, others are just right for the handyman. Located in a transitional neighborhood this is an incredible investment opportunity with tremendous up-side potential. Get in on the ground floor, be part of the action. This is not for the faint of heart but promises unlimited excitement for the savvy, motivated investor. Opportunities like this come only once in a lifetime. Act now. Call today for more information.

3

CHILDREN OF GOD

LITTLE
BOOTS

THE BOOTS WERE A BRIGHT PATCHWORK of yellow, red, blue, and green. The boots that had been running and jumping and playing were now still. Small feet in blue socks that had been running in the yard were now still, too. The boy wore a matching sweatsuit in pastel greens and blues decorated with a frog and a pocket on the front. I always liked pockets. I used to collect rocks in my pockets. I wondered what he collected in his. The sweatsuit was the outer layer protecting against the desert winter wind as he played with his brother in the yard. Beneath it were several layers of multicolored T-shirts, extra insurance against the biting cold. One shirt said rugby; one had pictures on it, cartoonlike figures with words written underneath in English. His hands poked through the soft, fleecy sleeves. The hands, like his feet, were quiet, not grabbing everything in sight as one might expect for an eighteen-month-old. His pacifier was a pendant hung at the ready around his neck.

The boots were surprisingly clean. The sweatpants had a stain on them, a hint of red. The sweatshirt had a twig stuck to the front as if the frog was holding it and putting it into the little pocket. The fleecy shirt was blotched with extra color, and the hands were stained as well. What was left of his face was beautiful, peaceful. The right side of his head was blown open, brain exposed, skull in jagged disarray. His left eye was closed, and you could still see his nose and mouth. Strangely, his features weren't distressed. In fact, if it weren't for the gaping hole and the blood all over, you could pretend he was just sleeping.

No notice had come over the radio, but that was the way it went all day long. Some days were like that. It was late afternoon, early evening. We had radio notice on the first two patients and the rest kept trickling in by ones and twos. It was not unusual to be without any official confirmation of inbound patients. Soldiers from the Iraqi Army had rushed in the back door of Al Taqqadum surgical. Someone yelled out, "Pediatric patient!" In their arms was the limp body of a little boy, blood-stained bandages wrapped around his head. *Damn!* The kids are always the worst. It just seems more unfair, and it seems to touch deep nerves in everybody. The boy whimpered once or twice. That was a good sign, I supposed. He still had a sense of and response to pain. There was no parent around—his parents were busy. His dad lay wounded four beds down in the ER. His mom was saying good-bye to Mohammed in the back room. His little sister was being entertained by Iraqi Army soldiers in the lobby. We had no name for the little boy. He was John Doe for the time being. Admittedly it was an odd place-holder name for a little Iraqi boy, but it worked for us. The kid was probably six at the oldest, just the age of my own little Andrew. The doctors worked hard. Who knows how it will ultimately turn out? He had a penetrating head wound, presumably with shrapnel still lodged inside. That is never a good thing. In the best of circumstances it would be hard and require surgeries, rehabilitation, and luck. But in Iraq, a war-torn world, there won't be the surgeries or the rehab, and most days here luck runs a little thin. It did for this family today. What this family has, what the people and the country have, is their faith. Will it be enough?

Twelve to fifteen Iraqi Army guys were gathered in the lobby, talking and waiting. A small two-year-old girl sat on a wooden bench dressed in a denim pantsuit. The suit was dark blue with highlights of pink, with the word "Jeans" printed across the top of the left pocket. I wondered what this little girl collected in her pockets. I soon found out. One of the Iraqi soldiers stuffed pieces of candy in each one. It occupied both of them for a moment. It gave everyone in the lobby something to smile about. We needed that. The girl had at least four pockets, and soon each was filled to the bursting point. The sweets and treats would come in handy later. She didn't know it then, but she would need a lot more than candy.

She was oblivious to how her world changed that afternoon. Someday she would know the story of her brother Mohammed, but for the short run she will see and sense the shift in her mother and in her father . . . if he survives. What candy the Iraqi soldier didn't stuff into her pockets he fed her. She sat quietly on the wooden bench, licking a small chocolate candy bar. She smiled at the soldier as he talked to her. I pointed and smiled at her shoes, Mary Jane—style leatherette, with a small strap and buckle across the top of the foot. But instead of the traditional black, her shoes were a lovely hot pink with bling on the top, a round

THE SWEATPANTS HAD A STAIN ON THEM, A HINT OF RED.

circle of metal and jewels. They sparkled. I said, "Your shoes are great. I love the color. I love the sparkle." She gave me a funny look. She was a little shy at first and, of course, clueless as to what I was saying. But I kept pointing to her shoes and smiling. Pretty soon she smiled back. Then I lifted my shoe up next to hers; she looked at my combat boot, she looked at me, and she smiled. She got it. We laughed. Sadly, our fashion show was soon cut short.

By now the girl's hands were gooey with chocolate. The soldier wiped them with a quick once-over and then turned to talk with the others. She still had chocolate all over and in between her fingers. I started wiping them again. We made it a game. I cleaned one finger and stopped. Then I looked for more. She caught on and started pointing out the chocolate to me. Her little hand fit neatly in mine. I bent down and kissed it. She giggled. Iraqi men in uniform were still all around. The little girl was given to the guy with three stars on his shoulder, a colonel in the Iraqi Army, I think. She was going to ride home with them. Mom was just a little too busy right then to look after a three-year-old. She had other things on her mind: one child killed, one fighting for life, a wounded husband, and another child dead two months ago. Preparing to fly by helicopter to Balad with her wounded six-year-old who needed more care, the mother left her only remaining child in the hands of the Iraqi Army. With sketchy directions scratched on a small piece of paper from someone's notepad, they headed into the darkness. Sure the Humvees had GPS, but it isn't quite the same as inputting a local address

THERE WAS NO PARENT AROUND— HIS PARENTS WERE BUSY.

into a Lexus or BMW and following well-maintained streets lit with bright lights to a quaint, upscale neighborhood by the lake. Instead, it was a moonless night and they were traveling unmarked roads filled with potholes, potholes often filled with improvised explosive devices. But there was little choice. They had to find their way to her house and to the extended family members who were at home, waiting and wondering.

If the little girl with her pink shoes looked out of place amidst the Marine Corps green décor and the camouflage ensembles worn by everyone else, her mother stood out even more. The woman wore a beautiful black embroidered dress with a long skirt and long sleeves. The bodice, the sleeves, and the skirt all had black needlework accents. Subtle texture, black on black, gave the dress richness and depth. Her embroidered scarf was a beautiful deep maroon, almost a blood red. It wrapped around her head and draped across her shoulders and fastened in front with a pewter-colored pin. The woman was beautifully dressed. She could have been going shopping or to an early dinner at a favorite restaurant with friends, or maybe to catch an evening show. I wish she would have been.

The woman couldn't have been very old, but she looked tired and wrought. Wisps of brown hair poked from beneath the scarf. Her brown eyes were red and swollen. As impeccably as she was dressed, her dress looked a little crumpled and a little stained, especially on the left shoulder. The stains were neutral in color, mixed with a little hint of red. One could imagine she'd brushed against or leaned into something. And indeed, in the truest sense of the word she had. The stains on her dress were bits and pieces of Mohammed's brain and spatters of his blood.

She spoke no English, but one didn't need words to know she was in anguish. Tears flowed freely; she beat herself her on the head and chest with both hands as she wailed. One needs no translation for the grief of a mother. I stood beside her and simply put my arm around her. I was helpless and horrified, and at the same time I was honored to be a witness. It doesn't get any more real than this: real life and real death in a war zone. Silently I watched the scene: a mother saying good-bye to her baby . . . a mother praying, crying in anguish to Allah . . . a mother kissing her baby's face . . . a mother gazing at her baby's face one last time . . . a mother in shock, not wanting to leave, wishing it could be some other way. She reached out and held the child's hand one more time, kissed the chubby fingers that surely had always been reaching and grabbing.

"Why didn't I die? Why not me? Why my children? It should have been me. Why didn't Allah take me?" One hardly needed a translator to understand the words. One certainly needed no translator to understand the depth of the pain and utter anguish. There wasn't much time to grieve, not much time to say good-bye, not much time to hold that hand. She had to turn her attention elsewhere.

The mother made her way to the ER and I stood with her at the end of John Doe's bed. She was praying to Allah. I lifted my hands in prayer, too. She seemed to understand I was joining her in prayer. We said good-bye in the ER as she prepared to fly to Balad with her son and her wounded husband. I gave her a hug. I held her close and tight and she held me in return; harder and harder we hugged. Her chest heaved and her sobs grew and grew. She had two dead babies, one fighting for life, and one left in the care of the Iraqi Army. We wept. Mother to mother, we grieved for the babies.

Mohammed died today. Did anyone notice or care? A few did. As the world watches and waits for the big news of the day, will it matter to him or his family whether Saddam dies today or years from now? Does it matter to him what the politicians in America decide to do in his country? It certainly mattered to him what they ting our service members die in vain, but what about Mohammed? He shouldn't die in vain, either. But what does that mean?

A child's photo anywhere in the world is a memory of the past or the hope of the future, even more so in Iraq.
Some stories shared around a hospital bed started by showing family photos pulled from a wallet.
Here a proud Iraqi Dad shows off his kids.

NEW YEAR'S DAY

WE SAT TOGETHER IN THE DIRT and leaned against the concrete wall of the rectangular mobile bunker just outside the Al Taqqadum surgical emergency room. Carried on the tide of hidden currents, smoke from her cigarette swirled and rose like holy prayers ascending to the heavens from the faithful. We were the faithful. The old woman and I sought answers and comfort from God and from each other. It was just the two of us sitting shoulder to shoulder. The silence spoke volumes. The silence was interrupted periodically by chantlike prayer that came in gasps between her sobs. The ordinary became sacred space. It was a simple makeshift temple—nothing fancy, no stained glass, no candle holders, no incense holders. No one was in charge of the service. We were accompanied only by the Spirit and the deepest cries of the human heart.

It was afternoon. A light breeze blew. The smoke shifted, blown off course and out of the tight river like streams in the sky. It blew around and across my face. It was a familiar smell. Smoke is usually an irritant, but today it was unusually pleasant. I breathed deeply and savored the sweet fragrance of the prayers ascending. The woman held out her cigarette and offered me a puff. I smiled, shook my head, and said, *"Shukran."* She seemed to understand. The smoke pit sometimes doubled as our hospital chapel, our private temple. It wasn't the first time. Sometimes it was the outdoor conference room; sometimes it was a counseling room, a place to talk with Marines and sailors. Sometimes, like today, it was a meditation room.

Who was this woman sitting next to me? What could I say? What could I do? The answers were strangely obvious but not necessarily easy to accept. I had no idea who she was. There was nothing I could say. There was nothing more I could do than simply sit with the old woman and be with her, absolutely present in the moment, sharing her pain and grief. We were out of control and helpless and left without the normal ways of communicating.

Sitting cross-legged in the dirt, arms wrapped tightly around each other, we wept together. Tears rolled down my cheeks as her pain washed over me; wave after wave hit her and splashed onto me. She wailed. She lifted her head and hands skyward. Her eyes pleaded, and so did her hands. Her Arabic words pleaded. Periodically I heard the one word I could understand: "Allah." As if on cue from a pre-rehearsed or ancient ritual, I spontaneously responded. I, too, lifted my head and tear-stained eyes. I lifted my hands. I repeated the mantra, "Allah." She nodded her approval. She knew that I understood. And so we continued: smoking, chanting, praying, pleading, and weeping. We would have sat there longer but, as if following some unwritten schedule, she knew time was up. She crushed the cigarette into the dirt, the only physical evidence left of our time together. But she knew. I knew. Allah knew. Now she needed to know something else. She needed to know what was going on in the ER.

Her family had been hit and wounded. It didn't matter whether they'd been hit by mortars or IEDs; the results were the same. Her sister was hit in the face, eyes swollen shut, maybe one blown away. Her sister's husband was hit too. The nieces and nephews—was it two or three, or was it four? It all begins to blur: leg wounds, arm wounds, head wounds.

Who had what, and who knows why? Would they live or would they die? I don't speak Arabic but I know those were her questions as she moved from litter to litter in the ER, trying to understand what happened and make sense of it. Another sister had survived the attack and hovered around the ER, too. Periodically they stopped and met in the middle, to talk, compare notes, and commiserate. I followed their lead. It was their dance. The doctors, nurses, and corpsmen were busy. The two Iraqi women, the two translators, and I moved and darted in between. Litter to litter, patient to patient, family member to family member, we stopped to hug, to weep, to wail, to pray, to hope. In the background, the doctors called for medication, the nurses called for assistance from the corpsman, the monitors beeped, and the Marines stood by as security and waited for word to call the helicopters for transport. Across the dull roar of the busy ER the call rang out. "Nine line's been dropped. Be here in ten minutes." Last-minute preparations for transport were made.

An unexpected trip to the ER on any day anywhere is bad. In a war, it's worse. The two Iraqi women looked old and tired. I suspect even a good day in war will do that, and today was not a good day. It was hard to know how old they were . . . forties, fifties, maybe sixties? Their long dresses were simple but attractive. One wore black. The color, unfortunately, was appropriate; we weren't sure how many of the wounded would survive.

It was time to say good-bye. The old lady and I held each other in a long embrace. She squeezed tighter and held on. She talked as though I knew exactly what she was saying. I responded by hugging her tighter and I repeated my mantra, "Allah, Allah, Allah." She squeezed me tighter. It was final this time; we had to let go of each other. She had to go. The patients were ready and the Marines waited quietly to escort her to the helicopter. She looked into my eyes and held my face between her hands and again said something as though I understood. I did. I nodded and said, "Allah." She smiled, nodded, and patted my face. I followed her to the flight line and watched her walk into the belly of CH-46. She turned to wave. I waved back. From the distance our eyes met one last time, but my heart is linked to hers forever.

AN
ANGEL

"**D**O YOU REALLY THINK THE SPIRIT OF GOD IS WORKING in my life?" she asked. I was stunned by the utter simplicity and sincerity of the question. For a moment I was speechless. Tears welled in my eyes and I simply nodded yes. I wondered sadly how anyone could think the Spirit of God is not working in her life.

I think she was puzzled by my response. She wants to study and learn and understand the facts. She wants to sort it all out. I've been there before. It's one reason I went to seminary. No doubt learning doctrine, dogma, and systematic theology has value and merit, but as I learn more, and more specifically as I live and grow, I am struck more and more by the mystery that is life, the mystery that is Spirit working in us.

"You know I wanted something more. I know there is something more. I want something comfortable for me, right for me, something that will make me feel safe inside." I stared at the young Iraqi woman sitting with me in my simple office in the little wooden chapel at Taqqadum. "Oh my God," I said to myself as I marveled at her incredible story. Here was a woman willing to risk persecution or execution not only because she worked for the Americans as a translator, but because she chose to become a Christian. She made the decision several years earlier as a student in Baghdad. Some of her closest school friends were Chaldean Christians and she felt drawn to the faith. She wanted to proclaim her faith publicly but had been warned against it by her friends, the priest, and her own intuition. It was too dangerous. She had not told anyone on the base. She was alone in her belief and practice until she met me and took the chance. We met weekly to study and talk, unless schedules were interrupted by the wounded or the dead or the fact that sometimes she was dead tired from having spent the night in the emergency room translating between her people and our doctors. I found an Arabic Bible sent by a church in the United States and gave it to her. She was thrilled. She felt connected.

She was young and isolated. Her religious decision made disconnection from her people and her family almost certain and the rest of her future terribly uncertain. The strange paradox for A'dab was that she was now in great danger outside the wire in her own country. Yet, she said, "I somehow feel safer now that I've taken the first step to meeting Jesus."

It was startling for me to distill my faith and my spiritual journey down to its essence and try to communicate it cross-culturally. But as I tried, I realized that it really remains so simple. I have distilled it to four words: connection and flow, love and gratitude. Connect with God, self, and others. Move in the mystical flow of life relying on Spirit to lead and guide. Ultimately live in a spirit of love and gratitude. I could not burden her with the fine points of dogma, doctrine, and theology, although I warned her that many well-meaning people would try.

Instead, I simply encouraged her to read about the life of Jesus. I also shared with her the advice that I got one day from a fellow engineer when I worked at General Dynamics. When in doubt about what that means or if confused, find a red-letter edition of the Bible and read the words in red.

How do you explain the books of the Bible? Well, it's simple. To the question of who were Matthew, Mark, Luke, and John? They were guys who for whatever reason recognized that Jesus was different and seemed a little more connected to God than most. Eventually they wrote down their stories about what happened.

> **"I SOMEHOW FEEL SAFER NOW THAT I'VE TAKEN THE FIRST STEP TO MEETING JESUS."**

The word "Gospel" simply means good news, and to me the amazing thing, the truly good news, is that we can have that same connection to God that Jesus did. We, too, can live our lives the same way. In fact, in my understanding, the Bible stories are still being written today. Each of us is in the process of writing our own gospel according to "fill in the blank with your name." I told her that. "You are at the beginning of your story. You are writing the opening chapters, especially if you begin to journal and record your thoughts, feelings, insights, and life happenings. You are writing the Gospel according to A'dab." I sat in amazement and my eyes welled with tears as I recognized the incredible and unpredictable move of the Spirit. I said to her, "I can envision the opening paragraph of your story. . . . Born during the middle years of the reign of Saddam Hussein, during a period of war in an ancient land whose history is marked by war, A'dab lived a comfortable life in the capital city of a great Middle Eastern nation. She was educated, and perhaps as a foreshadowing of what her future held in store, she paid more attention than other students during high school English classes. Although she was unaware, the Spirit was already preparing and working in her life. Divine appointments were already set."

A'dab was a young girl when she and her family lived in the capital city during a ten-year war with their neighbors to the east. That war was followed quickly by another war with a great nation from across the globe. She lived through a time of increasing deprivation. In essence it was another war, a ten-year war, an internal war for survival as the people struggled against the heavy yoke of an embargo. Everyone was hopeful during a brief period of peace. But the peace was short-lived under the reign of their increasingly cruel leader. It was only a matter of time before the great power from across the globe returned again, and so, too, did war. Although her country was in shambles and back at war, she was glad. She still had hope. She sought God with all her heart and embraced what little opportunity there was, and day by day began working, trying to bring peace to her land. But more than peace in her country, she sought peace in her soul.

A'dab will write her own Gospel story. Who knows how it will end? But it has a pretty good start. Wars, intrigue, secrets, life and death, hope and despair, faith and serendipities some would call miracles or say shows love and Spirit at work. We reviewed and marveled at the developing story. I hoped she believed just how amazing it was. She would need all the encouragement she could get in the months and years to come. There were sure to be bleak and difficult days ahead at TQ and eventually off the base. Her job was tough. She had English language skills, but nothing had prepared her for the carnage she saw daily in the ER. Inside the wire she was safe, with a steady job and people who cared. Outside the wire her life was threatened.

I'll probably never see her again, but I still wonder and worry about A'dab. There is very little I can do but trust that the same God who brought her this far will bring other people and situations across her path to see her through and ultimately write another great Gospel story filled with hope and faith.

SUMIA,
OUT OF TIME

THE SOFT, STEADY WHIMPER WAS HAUNTING. The wounded child had no understanding of what was going on. There was no comfort to be found. Was it a physical pain, was it a psychological wound, was it a spiritual cry, or was it all of that and more? No one knew. Gently, tenderly, the man cradled the little creature to his chest. Speaking words of comfort, compassionately stroking her hair, he looked lovingly at the limp little body he held in his arms. He rocked and murmured, half talking and half lullaby, and he struggled in agony, too. His young brow was furrowed beyond his years. He probably wasn't even thirty yet, but every year showed double on this day. His light brown eyes could not hide the weariness. He'd been traveling. He wasn't that far from home, maybe fifteen miles at most, but home might as well have been a thousand miles away. His face was thin and drawn, a fact barely hidden behind his neatly trimmed dark mustache and beard. He was neat and clean, but it was clear that fashion consciousness was the farthest thing from his mind. The color and style and coordination of his traveling clothes were the least of his worries. His collared T-shirt was an odd orange color. It wasn't that it was a bad color; in fact I rather liked it. It was just different. The navy-blue designer Nike running sweats it was paired with made an interesting combination. Convenience, comfort, warmth, and availability were obviously more important than fashion. It was December, and the Iraqi desert was especially cold at night.

One could feel the weariness and despair in the air. Everyone was tired. Everyone had plenty on their mind: blood, guts, gore, and more. It was hard to forget and it was harder still to know that at any time, more could come through the door. The guys on Ward Two were particularly tired today. They'd been up nearly all night. The suffering creature spent the night there and whimpered and cried almost constantly.

We shared the lakeshore with Sumia and her family. Our base was on one side and they lived in a small village on the other side of Lake Habbaniyah. The lake used to be enjoyed by Baghdad residents for weekend getaways and honeymoons. Now people just try to survive. It's too late for Sumia, but maybe her friends and future siblings will have a better chance.

Peace was elusive, even with our best efforts. We knew that. We felt hopeless, helpless, sad, and angry—a combination of all those feelings and more. We were separate, but united in the unanswered questions and collective pain. The language barrier was high but we all sat together, experiencing the effects of war up close and personally. We sat for a while in silence. Aimer, a patient and an officer in the Iraqi Army, was there. He was our language bridge. His self-taught English was pretty good. But in reality there was no need for words; this was beyond words. So I just sat for awhile with the man who was rocking and murmuring. His eyes were closed. My eyes were closed and I held my hand just above the little creature's head and silently prayed for healing, for relief, for a miracle, for a world that was some other way. Aimer followed my lead. He grabbed his Koran devotional book and held it to the little creature's head, hoping like I did for some relief to the suffering. We sat together murmuring and rocking, hoping and praying.

> THEY'D BEEN UP NEARLY ALL NIGHT. THE SUFFERING CREATURE SPENT THE NIGHT THERE AND WHIMPERED AND CRIED ALMOST CONSTANTLY.

Shot through the head while playing outside her home a month before, three-year-old Sumia would never be the same. One little girl was symbolic of so much. Did we do any good in caring for her, besides prolonging her agony and the inevitable? In a war-torn country with great innate riches but now impoverished, how will a kid with a shunt in her head and a feeding tube in her gut survive? Shunts and tubes need care. Feeding tubes need to be fed the right stuff and shunts need to be kept clean—all things not readily available in a small western Iraqi town, or anywhere in Iraq for that matter.

Sumia's dad was a poor man. He was a simple farmer living in a little village on the other side of the lake. Sumia had a little brother at home. Her mother was pregnant with another little brother or sister due sometime in the spring. Sumia needed ongoing, periodic medical care. She and her dad were on their way home from Balad, a place with a bigger, better-equipped hospital. They came via our base at Al Taqqadum. There was only one way home: by helicopter and then via convoy. It was the same each time she came through. There were shunt problems and feeding tube problems, and the tubes needed to get restocked with "food." By convoy and helicopter, they came and they went. What happens when we eventually leave? Unfortunately we all know the answer to that question, and so we come back again to the unanswerable questions, such as did we help her?

Would it have been better to make her comfortable and let her wounds take their natural course in a couple of days? Now instead she'll die in a couple of months, or maybe in a couple of years. In the meantime her father, a poor farmer, will struggle to make the periodic journey to Balad. It is a pilgrimage for him, and he hopes his efforts and faithfulness will reward him with a medical miracle. He needs one. She needs one. Bright and vibrant, three-year-old Sumia had been walking and talking, doing what three-year-olds do: learning colors, learning numbers, playing with toys, and periodically getting underfoot. What a pleasant distraction that would be now! Instead she lay helpless, moaning and whimpering, with the ability of a four- or five-month-old baby. Her pain radiated outward until it enveloped us all. It was hard to witness, but we did. We rocked and murmured, hoped and prayed.

Yes, I guess we did some good. We tried. We showed care and compassion. In turn we hoped the message of care and compassion would spread to some of the people in some of the places around TQ, in the towns and villages of Al Anbar province. Though I couldn't understand the Arabic, it was obvious that the Iraqi men in our hospital ward cared about this little girl and her dad. We gave compassion, and in turn gave the opportunity for others to do so too. And in that sense, Sumia's dad was a rich man. We gave a father a few more precious nights to cradle and rock Sumia, his little girl, to murmur and sing her lullabies. And maybe, little by little, care and compassion spreads one person at a time, one family at a time, one neighborhood at a time. Unfortunately we may run out of time before the job is finished. In the meantime, little Sumia and so many like her are caught in the crossfire. They are out of time.

BRIGHT ORANGE BUCKET

A trip to the Home Depot will never be the same for me. The bright orange bucket decorated with a few words and a simple picture is a recognizable symbol of a great American company. Everybody's seen the five-gallon Home Depot buckets; they are the must-have sturdy, useful, standard implement around the house.

It was the same in Iraq. The bright orange buckets were multifunctional equipment for us at the hospital. They were impromptu stools when seating was in short supply, and it was always in short supply waiting for patients to arrive via helicopter or ambulance as the team gathered in the emergency room. You might even say they were decorations, too. When they were not being used they sat at the end of the emergency room beds, adding color to the otherwise military drab gray-green equipment set against institutional white walls. These buckets were the repository for personal articles and effects as the patients were laid on the beds to be prepped for medical care. It usually happened so fast. Everything was stripped off and thrown in the orange Home Depot bucket at the end of the bed. The contents were usually ripped, torn, blasted and bloody, dusty and sweaty—boots, helmet, flak vests, clothing, and personal items. Dog tags sometimes dangled over the side.

THE COPS,
THE TEACHER, AND
THE BEANIE BABIES

I LOOKED AROUND THE ROOM. These were the faces of the old Iraq. These were the faces of the new Iraq. The hopes and dreams of a nation rested on men just like these. Could they do it? Were they up to the task? They were wounded and weary, and sometimes outside the wire they ran low on supplies and spirit, but what choice did they have but to keep on keeping on?

Surrounded by wounded Ramadi cops and wounded Iraqi Army guys, the wounded schoolteacher and the piles of Beanie Babies sent by caring Americans, I knew I was helping to create a new Iraq one person at a time. Would it be enough? In reality, no, but it was better than nothing. The task was daunting. But we all were doing what we could for the cause.

Together we dreamed of a new Iraq. In our quiet moments together we hoped. In our quiet moments together we despaired. I really had no idea what the old Iraq was like, so how could I presume to envision a new Iraq? But these guys knew. This was their country. Had we made it better? Had we made it worse? The answers to those questions, with the advantage of time and space and that ever pesky hindsight, will eventually unfold. History years from now will pass judgment on the bigger picture. And yes, I was part of that larger scene, but for now my world and my role in creating a new Iraq was very limited.

I looked at Ahmed, the schoolteacher, lying wounded in bed. He'd been through a lot in the past week. I think most of the wounded Iraqis appreciated the care and the respite afforded by their stay with us. Ahmed was one of those who by the twist of circumstances ended up on our doorstep and stayed awhile. Although he knew no English, I visited him regularly. Aimer explained who I was, and so Ahmed had become part of my Reiki practice. I don't know whether these guys were just pleasing Aimer or me or whether they really believed in prayer, but for a few weeks in January, I was doing Reiki on five or six wounded Iraqis every night and together we hoped for healing.

Ahmed was in his final year of training. He wanted to teach the children, to educate the new Iraq. He himself was young, not yet twenty-one. I looked at him surrounded by Beanie Babies, critters of every color of the rainbow set against the dark olive-gray-green military blanket, and I had a vision. I saw the new Iraq. My dream, my hope, my prayer, is that Ahmed, the young teacher, will survive the violence and become a key player in building a new Iraq in his neighborhood in Al Anbar province. I will never know for sure whether this will happen. But if he does survive, year after year he will touch the lives of students and their families.

I know it was a silly thought, a long shot, a dream far beyond logical reality. The task is so big. Iraq is a country of about thirty million, and my young schoolteacher friend would touch at most probably thirty-five kids per year. It would take a lot of years, many lifetimes, at that rate. It was too late for some of the little ones we'd seen, like eighteen-month-old Mohammed and three-year-old Sumia, who were caught and killed in the crossfire, but there were others waiting. But maybe, just maybe, the ripple effect of kindness and compassion given and received would take root, heal old wounds, and grow a new generation fresh and full of life somewhere near the banks of the Euphrates.

Ahmed almost died the night he was wounded, but he didn't. He survived and needs to keep surviving. For in my vision I see him year after year telling his story. In a region where support for America was mixed at best, I see him telling the story of living for a week or two with the Americans. In a region marked by deep tribal divides and long-held grudges, his students need to know how we cared for friend and foe alike and how we struggled to save life and limb, his included. In a world not known for religious tolerance, his students need to know how a female, American Christian was affectionately "adopted" by the Ramadi cops and the Iraqi Army guys in the hospital as their Imam, their spiritual leader. His students need to know how we worked together

> I SAW THE NEW IRAQ.
> MY DREAM, MY HOPE,
> MY PRAYER IS THAT AHMED,
> THE YOUNG TEACHER, WILL
> SURVIVE THE VIOLENCE
> AND BECOME A KEY PLAYER
> IN BUILDING A NEW IRAQ.

and prayed together for them, for the children, for the new Iraq. Aimer translated as I told Ahmed my vision. Ahmed was a quiet, soft-spoken guy. He smiled a shy smile and told Aimer to tell me, "Yes, I will remember. Yes, I will tell the stories. Yes, I will teach the children."

Ahmed left one day in late January. It was time for him to go. We sent him off still bandaged and still a little bruised. We sent him off with a bag a Beanie Babies slung over his shoulder, and I hope we sent him off with a little hope, too. It was a peculiar sight. I smiled and my eyes grew teary at the same time. I knew in my heart this was one of the men who would have an instrumental role in building a new Iraq.

I FEEL PRETTY

"I feel pretty, oh so pretty. I feel pretty and witty and gay. . . ." The words to the song suddenly popped into my head. How odd! In my mind, I flashed back to another time, wearing a long multicolored dress with puffy sleeves and a ruffle at the bottom. My hair was curled and fell below my shoulders and was pulled back with a big purple bow. Around my neck I wore a choker secured by a purple satin ribbon. I carried a mirror decorated with fluffy pink feathers and small pearls around the edge. I still remember twirling and dancing to the song, looking into the mirror, using it

as a prop, and I still think I was one of the prettiest. Girls from the third, fourth, and fifth grades all danced during the Spring Fling musical. I was in the third grade.

Today I was wearing shades of brown and tan, not nearly as colorful as my third-grade dance costume. Although I've always worn brown well, it's not my best color, but then again it's not my worst, either. I guess the point is, it wasn't my outfit that was making me feel pretty today. Hmm . . . sometimes it's just the little things that really make a difference. It did for me. The previous night I had dyed my hair. It wasn't the first time, but it was the

time and the place that made the difference. I was in the middle of Iraq in a shower trailer, dyeing my hair at midnight. Odd? Yes. Worth it? Absolutely, to wake up, look in the mirror, and start humming "I feel pretty, oh so pretty. . . ." In the middle of Iraq, in the middle of a war zone . . . yes, I'd say it was worth it. I sat on the wooden bench reading a romance novel in the shower trailer at midnight a tenth of a mile away from my room, and lest you think it only my imagination or ego singing to myself, the mind-body-spirit connection was reaffirmed by others. The next day at least two people commented. One said, "You look refreshed." The other said, "You look great." It was a testimony to how it all works together and how important attention to every area is key to maintaining balance.

Every day in Iraq, I take the time to put just a little makeup on; it makes the difference. I may not sing "I feel pretty" every day, but strangely I often look in the mirror here and think wow, I'm actually looking pretty darn good . . . happy, healthy, a little glow . . . but then again, who could help but look good? There is no other place I'd rather be than right here, right now, doing exactly what I am doing; it doesn't get any better than this. No wonder I feel pretty. Cammies or no cammies, makeup or no makeup, dust and dirt, long days and long nights, seeing the wounded and the dead, it was not a particularly pretty place, not a place particularly conducive to being pretty. Most say there is nothing pretty here, but pretty is all around in small ways—the blue sky, a little flower surviving and blooming, birds flying, a co-worker's happy face, but more than all that there is a pretty available all the time, the pretty that is within. And on this day it flowed.

HEAVEN IN
THE MIDST
OF HELL

ADVENT MEDITATION

"**I** WANT TO KNOW HIM . . . I WANT TO SEE HIM," the praise chorus from the church service repeated several times. It was a church service like any other. There was nothing special or fancy. It was the 1100 Sunday-morning general Protestant service held in a simple wooden building. The cheap plastic patio chairs were set neatly in rows. Each section on either side of the main aisle had six chairs. There was overflow seating on either side of the altar area. The place comfortably seats 150 or more; it was about one-quarter full. It was a predictable service: singing, prayer time, Scripture reading, a sermon, and more singing. There was no offering taken. There never was here.

The advent message about waiting for Jesus, like the rest of the service, was predictable. It was not necessarily a bad subject. But I found myself thinking beyond the narrow understanding of waiting for Jesus, wanting to know and see Jesus, waiting patiently, expectantly, and faithfully. Sometimes the messages get tired and worn, and so many assume that everything will be better sometime but really don't believe it can happen now. We are left to ask, but if not now, when? The standard answer is, "When Jesus comes." The praise song still rang like an ad jingle stuck in my head, "I want to see Him, I want to know Him." Is there any hope of finding Jesus in this war-torn country? Will our advent wait be rewarded? Will we see Him this Christmas? My mind flashed back to the night before.

The Al Taqqadum surgical ER was nearly overrun with patients. In the first round we received six; I never knew how many came in the second round. We were expecting at least five more. As the controlled chaos erupted, I stood like a wallflower at a dance. That's what I have to do at the beginning of every dance. Later, I'm usually invited to join in, or I watch and carefully make my way to wherever I'm needed.

The whole scene is an amazing sight. There is a flurry of activity. Sometimes it gets noisy. There are people moving, talking, and doing all kinds of things with sharp needles and instruments. Patients moan. Some scream. Sometimes the doctors and nurses get loud, too. Blood spatters. There are people giving drugs or putting patients under anesthesia. The dance is chaotic; the dance is orchestrated. It is both simultaneously. It is rehearsed, yet each time it is just a little different and spontaneous. We are dancers around each main person, the patient. Who has the lead? The patient? The doctor? The Spirit? Who knows? It is some grand circle dance. Maybe we each have a turn at leading the dance.

Like any good wallflower, I stood against the wall and tried to stay out of the way. There wasn't a lot of maneuvering room that night with eleven Iraqi patients waiting. But I still hoped to somehow participate, even though these were Iraqi soldiers and Ramadi cops who spoke no English. They probably didn't need me to pray Christian prayers in English. Then, one of the docs yelled, "Chaplain, come here!" I reacted, and he commanded, "Stand here; hold this guy's arm by his thumb." The doctor needed an extra set of hands to hold the arm so he could wrap the broken bones. Improvised explosive device blasts tend to break bones in arms and other places.

Arms are heavy when they just hang, when the person cannot hold his own arm up. Arms are heavy when you have to hold them just right, without moving, twisting, or bending or supporting them in any other way. I kept a firm grip on the patient's thumb. His arm hung like a motionless pendulum. I moved across the litter to the other side, reached over, and repositioned with a new grip. The doctor readied more wrap and casting material. I stood motionless holding the arm. It was hard to hold the heavy arm still.

I looked at the face of the Iraqi man. Earlier he'd been moaning. Now he slept peacefully. He could have been as young as twenty or as old as forty. It was hard to tell; war tends to age a person. I studied his face. He had a nice face with the fine, dark features characteristic of Iraqi men. A tube came out of his mouth. His chest rose and fell in a steady rhythm as the machine breathed for him. He had cuts all over his face: on the cheeks and nose, and around the eyes. There were nicks and cuts all over his body. But that was the least of his problems. He had a broken leg. It was an open fracture with visible bone fragments loose and floating around. He also had a broken arm, and who knows what else was wrong. He lay bare and exposed as the doctors worked to determine the extent of the injuries and stabilize him for transport. There was a lot going on. A doctor, a nurse, and a couple of corpsmen worked the length of the patient taking X-rays and a cursory sonogram, drawing blood, establishing an IV, giving drugs, intubating on one end and placing a catheter on the other.

All that was going on, but I gazed at his face. He looked so peaceful. If only it were true in his waking moments. The sad reality, however, is that war rages all around and he is now a broken man. Only time will tell whether his spirit is broken along with his body. But his actions speak louder than words ever could. He bears the scars of sacrificial giving. He hopes and believes and works for a better life for himself and his country. How many have the faith to follow his lead?

It was late one night in early December in Iraq. I remember Patient 1634. I held his broken arm steady as the doc wrapped him. I gazed on his sleeping face and realized I didn't have to wait for Christmas for Jesus to come. I had already seen him and held his hand.

KUMAR'S GIFT

KUMAR, A QUIET, HUMBLE INDIAN MAN, beamed with pride, as well he should. His work was beautiful. It was a simple wooden desk and chair made with care, and made simply because he wanted to share his talent and give to others. A bright red-and-white bow decorated the brand-new chair. Never has a piece of furniture been so appreciated. A fine piece costing thousands of dollars planned by professional designers, made of expensive rare exotic woods and built by master craftsmen, could not compare. In fact, I wouldn't want it. I like my desk and chair made from salvaged wood, nails and dowels still visible, without finish or paint. Even though it is simple, it has flair. Carefully cut and sanded corner pieces lend it strength and style. A shelf hidden underneath and out of the way adds a place for books and CDs. It is sturdy, rugged, stylish, and functional, but more important than the outward characteristics are the inward things. Most important, it was made by someone who wants to help, wants to please, and wants to give.

What can I give in return? A smile, a thank you? It seems so little for such a beautiful gift. It seems so little for the time spent on it for me by a total stranger. But through the desk, I am learning a lesson about gifts and about receiving them. It feels nice, but it feels odd. You don't always receive from the people you give to. I give and I give and I give of myself all the time in my job. I give the gift of myself, my time, my listening ear, my compassionate presence, and cannot ever expect anything in return. I often receive thank yous and many intangibles, such as the simple knowledge that I've helped somebody or made the world just a little better. But through the gift of the desk, the universe was giving me something tangible just because.

I'd love to ship my little desk and chair home when it's time to leave. But today as I received my gift I knew that even if it were physically possible, I could not. I will need to continue the cycle. I will give it as a gift to someone when I leave and it really will not be a gift from me, but from Kumar. It will continue his gift of care to someone else, someone destined to serve here for six months, twelve months, or more. It will be a desk used to write letters home, a place to read or study, a place to journal events, insights, and spiritual growth found here in Iraq. It might be a place to rest one's head for a quick ten-minute cat nap, or it could be used to hold a coffeepot or even a Christmas tree in December of 2007 or 2008 or beyond. Who knows?

> **WE COME TOGETHER AND BUILD A LIFE FOR OURSELVES, DAY BY DAY, AS WE TRY TO HELP THE IRAQIS BUILD THEIRS.**

In a place like this, where things are hard to come by and many people are good at scavenging, it would be interesting to catch up to this little desk and chair a few years from now. It was a simple desk and chair that came into being because I'd nonchalantly mentioned to my friend and Marine Corps Martial Arts Program partner, Thea, that I would love to have a table and chair in my room. She in turn mentioned it to a co-worker who loves spending his spare time building things, creating something out of nothing, creating useful pieces of furniture out of scrap, out of things that otherwise would be thrown away

or burned. Magically, within about three days my desk appeared. Ask and ye shall receive. And to that I simply say thank you.

Every day we were building community together, not only a physical place to live but a community to care about and take care of each other. We built tangible things via simple everyday items like a simple desk and chair, made from scraps. But we built intangibles, too. We all came here for our own reasons; some were ordered here and some volunteered. We all have our own personal agendas, but we come together and build a life for ourselves day by day as we try to help the Iraqis build theirs. Here we work together: Americans, Indians, Irish, some from parts of the old Soviet Union, many from Uganda, and a variety of others from places scattered across the globe, a mini United Nations. It works within the camp; too bad it doesn't work yet just "down the street," outside the wire. If only we could communicate and convince the people there to learn the lesson from Kumar's desk and chair: work with the scraps you have, pour your heart into your work, and give it away to a friend, a neighbor, or even a stranger just because you care. What a different place this would be! Thanks, Kumar.

KNOW YOUR PEOPLE

"I'm Jedi," he said as he gave me a big grin.

Playing along, I asked, "Really?" The corpsman and I had earlier finished talking with patients in the American and Iraqi wards and now we were whiling away the late evening hours, shooting the breeze. Topics ran the gamut, but at some point in the conversation I asked him about his faith.

I've heard a lot of things; nothing much surprises me anymore. Faith and spiritual expression are as individual as each one of us. His grin widened as he continued, "Yeah, really, I'm Jedi. It says so right here on my dog tags." Now I was really curious. Jedi is not one of the over 250 faith groups officially recognized by the Department of Defense, and technically dog tags are only imprinted with ones from the approved list. He grabbed his chain and the dog tags, pulled them over his head, and flopped them onto the patient's chart where he was making notes. "See, right there, it says 'Jedi.'"

We laughed and I shook my head and said, "Wow, Jedi! That's cool." I laughed again and commented as I looked at the allergy noted on his red dog tag, "That's a pretty interesting allergy."

He laughed, "Yes, Ma'am, and my friend has an interesting one, too. His allergy is to fat chicks." We laughed and talked some more, and he told me a little about the Jedi faith.

Faith is integral to who we are, yet it can be a lonely journey. One young female Marine was not only one of few women in her unit, but she carried an extra burden. Raised in a conservative Baptist home, she had converted to Islam several years ago as a young adult and then married a Catholic. I checked with her periodically to make sure she had time and space to worship. I offered to talk with her about her faith and her challenges. I would have liked to have known more about her personal journey. She was doing okay, or maybe she wasn't. I never really knew because she never opened up. Paradoxically, in an Islamic country she was isolated from others in her faith.

I had a variety of unexpected religious preferences under my care in Iraq. There were American service members who identified themselves as Muslim, Hindu, Wiccan, Jedi, Agnostic, Atheist, and No Preference, and many who described themselves as Spiritual but Not Religious. I am their chaplain, too. I may not practice or understand much about the specifics of a particular faith, but I encourage and advise all service members as they walk their own spiritual path.

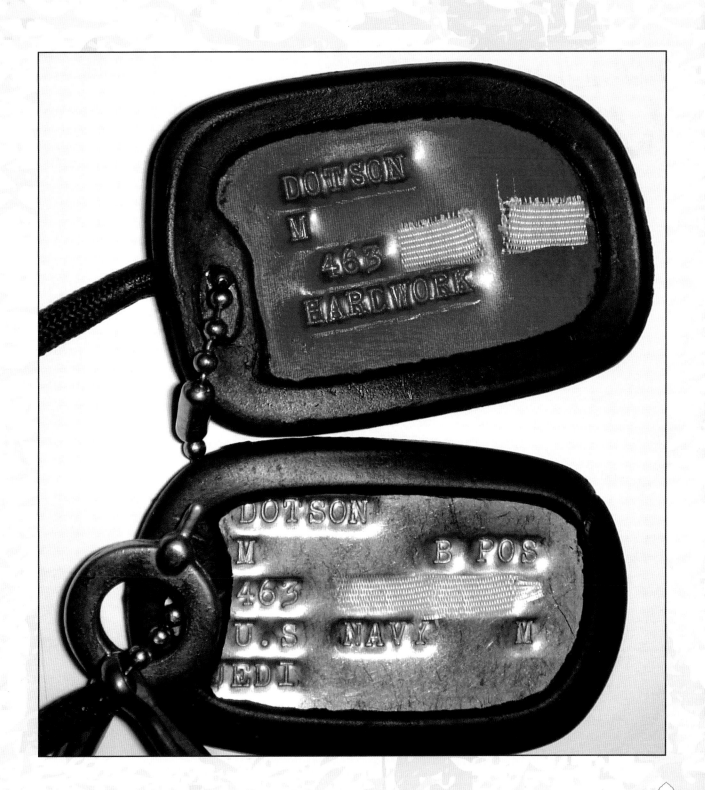

I'LL BE HOME FOR CHRISTMAS... MAYBE

A HALF MILE OUT, the driver turned the headlights off. We crept slowly down the busy road. As at any airport, parking was tight, and to the uninitiated the procedures looked like organized chaos. Thankfully we were with someone who knew the way. We parked on the side of the narrow dirt road, got out of the Humvee, and stumbled around in the pitch-black night. Our eyes adjusted, and murky shadows appeared. In the foreground we saw the dark outline of six small plywood buildings. Dim lights in the distance marked out the landing area. Periodically the door on one of the shacks opened and bright white light escaped. The check-in lines wound around and looped back on themselves. People murmured and muttered and did the bag-drag shuffle. It was dark and cold outside. The light and what little warmth there was needed to stay on the inside.

Crammed shoulder to shoulder, we managed our cumbersome packs and exchanged brief hellos. But no one was in the mood to chat. It was Christmastime, and as at any airport with flight delays, schedule hassles, and marginal weather, people were intent on getting where they needed to be. We showed our ID cards. The airport personnel had made the list and were checking it twice. We received our "boarding passes," which were actually coded letters and numbers written in black Sharpie pen on the back of our hands. Our waiting room was shed number five. Each shed housed people waiting for a different flight. Some of the sheds were filled to overflowing. It all depended on the popularity of the route and the size of the scheduled helicopter.

We were tired but not quite cranky—not yet, anyway. Now began the waiting game. There were no convenience stores or bookstores with snacks or reading material. In our shack there was a well-worn coffeepot that had been perking since early morning, and now it was almost early morning again. There was a cooler full of ice and bottled water. This was certainly a necessity during the summer heat, but not on a cold December night. Besides, no one wanted to drink too much; not now. No one needed to cool off and no one wanted to need a nighttime trip to the unlit port-a-johns, nor to try to "hold it" on the jiggly, rumbly helicopter ride. Some people had their own snacks: beef jerky, nuts, or candy. Some talked. A few read or stared into space, lost in their own thoughts. Still others slept.

AS THE MOON AND STARS DIMMED, WE KNEW THE LIKELIHOOD OF CATCHING A FLIGHT HOME FROM FALLUJAH TO TQ GREW DIMMER TOO.

There were three of us traveling together: me, my RP (religious program specialist), and the officer in charge of Personnel Retrieval and Processing. Two other guys, a Marine and a KBR contractor, wandered in to wait with us. We were happy to see them. There was plenty of room, and the extra body heat was a bonus. The cold, steady wind blew across the desert and assaulted and penetrated the uninsulated plywood shed. Periodically we peeked outside. There was a gathering gloom as the mist and clouds closed in. We waited. The minutes stretched into hours. We watched the clouds obscure the stars and play peek-a-boo with the moon. As the moon and stars dimmed, we knew the likelihood of catching a flight home from Fallujah to Al Taqqadum grew dimmer and dimmer, too.

We watched the clock strike midnight and we stretched out on the olive-green military cots, grateful for the long underwear beneath our cammies. Our jackets, gloves, and caps helped, too, but we still shivered in the cold. Sleep was light and fitful. We hoped someone would remember to get us if our flight came. Periodically we heard helicopters circle, hover, land, and take off. At least they were still flying. A little after 0130 we heard a helicopter fly by. Was it landing? No, it wasn't close enough. Were they circling? Maybe they'd come back around and land the second time. They came back, but then we heard them leave. We looked at each other. We knew what that meant. Soon it was confirmed. A Marine popped his head in the door and said, "Sorry, that was your flight. They can't land. Conditions deteriorated. No more flights tonight. Maybe tomorrow." And so we called our hosts, and sometime after 0300 we fell once again into our borrowed beds.

The same thing happened night after night. Three nights in a row we dutifully arrived for a 2300 showtime. We hung around, waiting and hoping, watching the weather change and listening for the welcome wump, wump, wump that never came. Three nights flights were cancelled. It was not uncommon this time of year for flights to be cancelled for a week or more. I thought of my daddy, who flew Navy helicopters forty years ago. I knew he and his buddies could have landed in these conditions. I knew these pilots today could, too. But rules are rules, and there was no emergency or critical mission hanging in the balance. There was no reason to push the envelope. We were just passengers needing to get from here to there. I just wanted to be home for Christmas. I knew when I went to visit my Marines in Fallujah a few days before Christmas that it might be a hard schedule to keep. Was I going to spend Christmas on the road or at home?

We took the quick route through the city of Fallujah on Christmas Eve morning. It was considered a risky option but it was much faster. Combat Logistics Battalion (CLB) 5 was making a morale visit to their guys serving in Habbaniyah and they offered me a ride home. This picture is taken out the window of the Humvee as we rounded the last corner and entered the homeward stretch. I was riding in the tenth and final vehicle.

Home for me this year was back at TQ. "I'll be home for Christmas, just you wait and see. I'll be home for Christmas, if only in my dreams." The words to the familiar Christmas carol ran through my head and had more meaning to me than ever before. I thought about home half a world away, where in a few days my five- and eight-year-old boys would grab freshly filled Christmas stockings and gather around the tree to open packages. I thought of my friends and co-workers at TQ, and I thought of my Christmas trees waiting in my room and office. The twinkly glow from the bright lights cheered me on cold, dark nights, even after the nights spent at the hospital or at PRP. As hospitable and welcoming as the people in Fallujah were, I didn't want to spend Christmas on the road.

After three nights of cancelled flights and the same weather forecast into the foreseeable future, I was beginning to despair. Then came an unexpected offer I couldn't refuse—or could I? There was a Christmas Eve convoy going from Fallujah to TQ and they could find us a couple of seats. Did we want it, yes or no? I looked at my RP. He looked back at me and said, "It's your call, Ma'am. It's a convoy, but it's our only chance to get home for Christmas." Without any more hesitation or thought, I said, "Yes, let's do it." We were headed home for the holidays.

Holiday travel can be hell. It's bad anywhere, but in Iraq travel anytime could get worse, much worse. Convoys going here and there, back and forth, never knew what danger lurked. Most made it to their destinations with no problem. Some did not. I knew too well what that looked like. Iraq was still a dangerous place.

I'd heard the Explosive Ordnance Disposal guys talk about route clearing. Day after day, night after night, they drove the roads around Al Anbar. Old Chicago, Fiesta, and Michigan were all roads I'd seen on a map. Soon I'd see them in person, all parts of the route through and around Fallujah but all parts of what at the time my EOD guys called the most dangerous road on the planet. But I'll be home for Christmas—maybe.

CHRISTMAS DAY

THE RADIO BLASTED THE CALL. "Attention, duty fire-strikers: we have one urgent surgical, by air, ten minutes, gunshot wound to face."

Our afternoon was interrupted. You were never sure what you would find when you got to the hospital. Sometimes the information coming in from the field barely resembled the reality of what walked through the door in terms of numbers, nationalities, or severity of wounds. Especially today, I was hoping the call would be wrong. I got to the hospital. *Damn!* I thought. The urgent surgical was in fact true. Here we go again; no warning, no rest even on Christmas. The double doors burst open. There was no time to evaluate the patient in the ER. He was whisked immediately down the passageway to the operating room. The patient, Dustin Kirby, was a severely wounded corpsman, hit by a bullet in the jaw. It looked bad.

I wandered between the operating room and the lobby, doing what I could in each place. On some days I was able to help in the OR in real, tangible ways by gowning, gloving, and masking up and being an extra set of hands to grab tools or equipment. This, however, was not one of those days. A couple of surgeons, the anesthesiologist, a nurse or two, and the dentist all crowded in one small space on the right side of the corpsman's head. Millimeters separated this patient from life and death. His life literally hung in the balance, dependent on the delicate, quick, precision maneuvers of the medical team. Blood loss was heavy and there wasn't much time. Blood was pumping everywhere, into the patient, out of the patient.

Today in the OR, I tried to help in intangible ways. I stood as a silent witness, watching, hoping, and praying. We needed a Christmas miracle. The epic struggle between life and death raged on in the OR and would for the next few hours. I wandered back to the lobby.

Two Marines sat on the simple wooden bench near the ER. These were the Marines on duty at the hospital. While the doctors and nurses were busy in the OR, the Marines cataloged the patient's personal belongings. Latex-gloved hands dug through the orange Home Depot bucket and pulled out items one by one. A bloody boot poked out the top and socks hung over the side. The small stuff fell to the bottom of the bucket: dog tags, a wallet, a small notebook. The second Marine clutched a clipboard and pen. He confirmed and documented each item and bagged everything in a clear plastic garbage bag. The bag would be sent with the patient to the next stop: the morgue, or follow-on surgical care.

The corpsman's flak vest was close by. It silently spoke volumes and told the story. Blood ran like rivers down the length in the front, back, and sides and had soaked deeply into the fabric covering the sapi plates. The blood still had a shimmery wet sheen. Fresh blood mixed with sweat, dirt, and fear has a smell all its own. A brown plastic spoon and a white thermometer were hooked in the front loops of the vest, and extra pouches contained other tools of his healing trade. The blood-spattered helmet lay on the gray floor nearby.

The normally brown flak vest was now a strange brownish blood red. It clashed with the red Christmas tree skirt in the corner. The little Christmas tree looked like an afterthought in this strange scene. There were only a few lights, a little glittery

The bloody flak and the Christmas tree in the hospital waiting room brought together clashing shades of red. The vest belonged to Dustin Kirby, a Navy corpsman from Georgia. He was given a Christmas Day miracle. He survived the direct gun shot to the jaw and has been featured in three New York Times *articles.*

tinsel, and a couple of ornaments. But the tree tried its best to brighten our mood. It was an unusual contrast. The Marines and I stared in silence at the tree and the vest. We were mesmerized by the perversity and the paradox. Finally one said quietly, "Shit! He took quite a hit. Damn! This guy just has to make it." The other one nodded agreement and said, "Yeah, it seems so unfair. He's a corpsman and it's Christmas. He's gotta make it." I silently nodded my agreement.

I walked from the lobby back to the OR. Life and death still wrestled. It was touch and go. I stood there a long time. There was not much left to do but whisper "Merry Christmas."

THE BUTTERFLY'S
REMINDER

I**T'S THE LITTLE THINGS IN LIFE** that can make or break you. Little things can make a bad day better or give the hope or hint of a silver lining in an otherwise cloudy day. Conversely it's the little things that can make what began as a good day turn bad. Yet so often we overlook the little things perhaps precisely because they are, well—little.

In the frenzy and focus on goals and accomplishments of real or imagined importance, we consider the little things unimportant. We think they don't count or add up to much. Many people don't ever give the little things much thought; they've become part of the invisible backdrop of life, part of the cacophony of background noise we learn to tune out. For those who do give them thought or attention they chastise themselves or "get it" from someone else: a coworker, boss, friend or spouse who accuse them of wasting time. They are told to refocus. The command can be subtle or overt, verbal or nonverbal: "Stay focused on the mission. Don't be distracted. Get the job done."

Yet I went to Iraq with an unproven theory regarding the importance of the little things in life. Intuitively I knew it was the little stuff that would help keep me balanced and maintain my sanity. It was really a statement of faith based on my own spirituality. I knew I had to pay attention to the little things and help others do the same. It was a paradox: while I sought heightened focus one of my goals was to find distractions. It was not merely to defocus or waste time but it was to find a purposeful distraction. The goal was real world, real time, meditation to bring heightened awareness of self, others and the environment. It was a way to connect with the present moment. What better spiritual goal and what better practical goal in a combat zone than heightened situational awareness?

There are many challenges in an intense environment. There is a constant struggle to find connection beyond the immediate need or crisis. Paradoxically there is the natural desire to protect oneself from a deeper awareness or connection. Many of the sights, sounds, and smells of war assault the senses and the sensibilities. The horror leads to a natural question: "Who wants to fully connect with any of that?" Therefore many people try to shield themselves from reality and in doing so they disconnect emotionally. Boredom, addiction to video games, movies, other mind numbing activities and glassy-eyed stares all show as symptoms. From time to time we all needed reminders of the beauty right under our noses.

Responding to a radio call one day an off-duty nurse stopped me and said, "Chaplain come here. Look at this." I looked at the ground where he was pointing. It was a beautiful orange-and-black butterfly. I smiled at him. He looked pleased. We had talked many times at lunch or dinner about many things. Doctrine, formal theology and conservative Christianity were his favorite topics. But in that moment none of the previous conversations mattered nearly as much as that one shared moment of magic. "Wow, that's beautiful," I said. "Thanks for stopping me and sharing it with me. I think I'll try to get its picture." The butterfly fluttered briefly, and we were afraid it would fly away before I got a chance to "shoot" it. But I was lucky that day. I was rewarded by the butterfly's reminder.

IN THE BLAST ZONE

"I almost got shot last night by a sniper. The bullets were whizzing by. You can actually hear the ripple in the wind. It was close between me and a part of the inside of the turret. Every time I would pop my head up he'd shoot. Yeah, that was kind of exciting, maybe even fun. But tonight I almost got blown up by an IED. Don't let anyone say there's anything exhilarating about that. It just hurt like hell. It was pretty weird; everything went into slow motion. It was an old IED hole, used before, cleared before . . . but we must have missed it. I saw the huge piece of concrete coming at me and then I felt it hit. It hurt. But I was lucky. I was close. It could have been much worse."

He'd pretty much said it all, so I just nodded and said, "Yes, you're right; we've seen worse here." And with that we spent some time in silence just thinking about it.

OUT OF
THE SILENCE

I T WAS MORNING, and it was the evening of my fortieth day in Iraq. For forty
days I had walked amidst the wounded and dead and those who care for them.
I had not yet cried. But I wept that day. I wept for three Marines killed three days
earlier, and for the one who died before my eyes that day. I wept for the others, too,
almost three thousand American dead and nearly ten times that number wounded.
And those are the wounds we can see and choose to acknowledge. How many more
are wounded in mind and spirit? The reality is that we are all wounded by war; we just
don't know it. I wept for all of us that day, me included.

"God damn this fucking war!" Were these words spoken by a Marine as a com-
mentary of his time in Iraq? Maybe, but sometimes I mutter the phrase under my
breath around here. Why? Because there are times when more eloquent expression
evades me and there is no time for lengthy prose when a simple mantra will do. The
sentiment fit the afternoon perfectly.

We were making last-minute preparations, and people were beginning to arrive at the chapel for the memorial service for the three dead Marines from MWSS 373. I was there to provide additional chaplain support. I knew there wasn't much I could do or say to make the situation better, but I was there to help, to be present, and if nothing else, to simply share in the grief. And then my radio went off: "Attention, duty fire-strikers: urgent surgical gunshot wound coming by air within twenty mikes [minutes]." Wonderful—a memorial service in progress and more incoming wounded or dead. Now do you understand my harsh sentiment?

This was one of those times when I literally needed to be in two places at once. So much for support at the memorial; I might be tied up for a while. I scrambled to the hospital. We waited for the patient. We never knew what was going to come through the door or when. Sooner was better than later, and we hoped for wounded and not dead. We hoped for salvageable. And so we waited not so patiently.

The thump, thump, thump got closer and closer. One begins to recognize the sound of the choppers as they near the hospital. Someone near the radio yelled out the obvious: "It's here." Someone else yelled out the warning, "CPR is in progress." We shot each other knowing looks. Not a good sign. The hospital corpsmen met the patient and unit corpsmen at the flight line and moved the patient from the helicopter to the back of a gator, a small utility vehicle. As we stood outside watching and waiting, we could always tell how bad the patient was by how quickly they flew off the helicopter and down the pathway that led from the flight line to the door of the Al Taqqadum surgical emergency room. Today they flew down the path and flung the ER door open.

Doctors and nurses rushed into action. Time was critical. Time was our enemy. The patient had been receiving CPR for at least ninety seconds, and we guessed in reality probably even longer. The pace in the ER was frenetic yet controlled and steady. They didn't have much time left. In fact, there was no time left to go down the hall to the OR. The doctors made the decision to cut through the patient's chest right there in the ER. The patient was hastily prepped: a razor ran quickly across the offending chest hair and the swish of a swab to disinfect the area followed. Brown iodine mingled now with bright-red fresh blood. The scalpel swiftly cut through the flesh as the surgeon struggled to expose and repair the damage.

Those of us not directly involved witnessed the unfolding drama in silence. It was obvious this guy was critical, as critical as they come. His life hung in the balance. There were two immediate questions. Would they find the problem in time? Would they be able to fix what they found? I think we all prayed right then, each in our own way. I stood close by but out of the way behind the third bed in the ER. Unlike other times, this time I didn't watch the struggle for life. Instead, I closed my eyes and listened and went inward, trying to connect with the patient and with the Spirit. Energy in the room was palpable. It was moving and flowing. I just hoped it would move in our favor. The doctors worked fast and furiously. Probably no more than ten minutes had elapsed since the patient landed on our doorstep.

The answer to the first question came. Yes, they found the problem. I opened my eyes to watch the evolving scene as the surgeon called out the answer to the second question. The older surgeon had sons of his own serving in combat with the Marine Corps. Today his hands were buried deep within the chest of a young Marine as he delivered the bad news: "The hole in his heart is huge. There is no way it can be repaired."

Someone else asked, "Is that it? Shall we call it?"

"Yes," was the reply, "call it at 1450." And just like that it was over.

The tension in the room was high. It wasn't a bad tension, although there was a roller coaster of emotion. It was first the emotion of expectancy and hope; then it was the emotion of letdown and lost hope. "Calling it" meant they'd declared the patient dead; there was nothing more they could do for him. More medical efforts to revive and repair him would do no good. We lost the battle that day. At least for this one, all hope was gone. He'd died of a broken heart. The bullet entered just where the sapi plates end in the flak vests. The shot went through his entire body. His heart was ripped in two. What other hearts would be ripped in two later that day, later that night, when they heard Mark is gone? Would it be those of a father, a mother, a sister, a brother, a wife, a child, a friend, a neighbor, a fellow Marine? Yes, it would be those and maybe more: a grandmother and a grandfather, an aunt and an uncle, a cousin, a childhood classmate. And really we all lost something that day when Mark's heart broke in two; our hearts broke a little, too. We wept.

Stunned at what I'd just witnessed in the ER, I walked back to the chapel and the memorial service in progress, muttering my more-than-appropriate "unchaplainly" mantra. I was over an hour late, but I arrived in time to hear some of the final remarks. Then I sat in silence, awash in the sea of grief for over an hour watching the Marines say good-bye. Several hundred people sat, others stood; all were silently and reverently waiting. Though no one spoke, there was a growing tension in the air. We waited in silence for an hour and fifteen minutes. We would have waited for as long as it took. I wish it had been a simple Quaker meeting, and in a broad sense it was. We met in a simple wooden building with simple chairs and simple benches. We gathered and were meditative and prayerful. Each sought to connect with one another and with God.

Yet this was no ordinary Quaker meeting. This was the end of a memorial service, a tradition, a ritual and final tribute where Marines in a combat zone say good-bye to fellow Marines killed in action. It is the moment when each Marine stops for a brief time of reflection in front of the boots, helmet, dog tags, and rifle of his fallen comrade and prays and pays final respects. With this final good-bye, the formal remembrance is finished. The warriors know that their friends are gone forever but that they must go forward and fight another day. They adjust their own armor—their mind, body, and spirit—hoping it's strong enough to protect them, and then they move on. After a brief pause in the high tempo of combat, they are back at. Later today or tomorrow they will be on the road again, facing sniper fire or IED blasts like the one that killed their friends.

One by one, the young men and women paused in reverential silence before each of the three photographs. They were lost in their own private thoughts, yet they were bound together in the communal warrior ritual. Many kneeled. Some stood. Some made the sign of the cross. All bowed their heads in prayer. Many reached out and touched the dog tags or held them and read them. Some placed their hands on the top of the helmets. A few ended by rendering a salute. Through it all, the faces in the photographs, memories of a better day, smiled bright and happy smiles in return. Some guys openly cried, others struggled to hold back the tears; some were stoic and showed no overt emotion. Surrounded by 350 grieving Marines and sailors, one couldn't help but be touched. Obviously, everyone was sad. Many were mad. Some were frustrated. Some wondered why. Others couldn't believe it was true. Some worried about their next mission; each one down deep inside knew it could have been them three days ago and it could be them three days or three weeks or three months from now.

Sometimes all we can do is remember, cry, and say goodbye. A final tribute for three of the fallen: A memorial service at TQ chapel for MWSS 373 Marines. Lance Cpl. Budd M. Cote, 21, of Marana, Ariz. Cpl. Matthew V. Dillon, 25, of Aiken, S.C., Lance Cpl. Clinton J. Miller, 23, of Greenfield, Iowa. All three Marines died December 11 while conducting combat operations in Al Anbar province, Iraq. They were assigned to Marine Wing Support Squadron 373, Marine Wing Support Group 37, 3rd Marine Aircraft Wing, First Marine Expeditionary Force, Marine Corps Air Station Miramar, California.

HEAVEN IN THE MIDST OF HELL

"YOU NEED TO REMEMBER GOD ALL THE TIME, not just when you are sick or tired or need help. Thank Him all the time for everything." The older man gave the admonition to the younger one. He was not quite old enough to be the guy's father, but it was sage advice. Separated in age by maybe fifteen years, he offered wisdom as an older brother might give to a younger one. They were separated, too, by a world of difference yet strangely and unexpectedly united, brought together by odd circumstances just three days earlier.

I sat watching the two men and smiled. I said in a teasing way, "Aimer, that's great; I couldn't have said it better myself. Wow! Preach it . . . you'll put me out of a job." He gave me a big smile in return and said, "Oh, no Ma'am . . . I just wish I could help David feel better." Now it was my turn to give a bit of sisterly wisdom: "You can, you do. We help each other." He started to protest, but I just shook my head and said, "Oh no . . . you do help." He took me seriously and literally, and said,

"Okay, Ma'am, just a minute. . . ." I was a little puzzled as he went to the deep stainless-steel sink in the corner of the room that served as one of the Iraqi wards in the Al Taqqadum hospital. Water dripped from the tall faucet and thudded as it hit the sink below. Aimer carefully washed his hands and face. It began to dawn on me what he was doing. He finished, turned, and slowly made his way back to the chair. He walked with a slight limp, an injury on his left ankle, a result of friendly fire from his time in Mosul two years earlier.

Aimer intentionally left his hands wet. He left a trail of water across the floor. It was better than the trail of blood that too many days marked the way down the passageway from the ER to the OR. Hands dripping, he walked directly to David and placed them on top of his head and began to speak in Arabic. David looked puzzled, but I knew that Aimer was praying. Aimer must have sensed the question as he paused and looked up after a few sentences as if to reassure and explain to David, "I am helping. I am asking God to help you."

Aimer went back to praying. I closed my eyes and lifted my hands toward heaven; my heart was full and I watched the scene in my mind's eye, transfixed and mesmerized in a moment of unity and oneness as we bowed together. I knew beyond head knowledge that I was witness to and part of a miracle. We were feeling it in our hearts and in the depth of our souls.

Four of us were sitting in a circle in a hospital ward, praying. We joined together, united heart to heart, connecting with each other and with God; loving and caring for one another, lifting one another to the heart of God. The spiritual power and presence was palpable; I tingled all over. There was no doubt. We were in the holy of holies, in the very presence of God.

The ordinary became extraordinary. There was nothing physical to announce the miracle, no physical flash of lightning, no earthquake. In fact, I am not sure anyone else saw or noticed what was happening in Ward Two. The football game blared in the adjacent room, permeating Ward One, and the corpsmen talked about their next assignments or problems with their girlfriends or bank accounts and bills. The TV in our room tried hard to distract, too. The World Wrestling Federation women's match played in the background on the Armed Forces Network. Scantily clad women showed lots of cleavage and gave new meaning to the phrase "high and tight," as their shorts barely covered their butts. They flung each other around the ring and glistened with sweat, grunted, and moved in some strange ritual that only wrestling fans seem to understand and appreciate.

Necessity is the mother of invention and nowhere is that more true than in a war zone. We made do with what we had. People found places and ways to worship wherever and with whatever we had. A room in an old crumbling building in Ramadi became the small Roman Catholic chapel, a place to refresh and reflect.

It was an odd temple indeed. While there was no spectacular immediate physical manifestation of a miracle, there was a shift in me and I think in all of us gathered there. Lightning struck the heart; an earthquake hit the soul.

Something shifted in the heart and soul of a young man who was wounded in mind, body, and spirit. There was a glimmer of hope for the young American who will carry forever the burden of killing an Iraqi child, a tragic consequence of the fog of war. Day after day he patrolled dusty, devastated streets and alleyways. He held buddies as they died. Eventually, under the influence of fear, adrenaline, and anger, rocks and grenades bear an uncanny resemblance to one another.

The hazel-brown eyes of the young American were windows looking into his soul. They gave us a perfect view of his weariness. His body showed it, too; he was beat. David sought solace, forgiveness, and rest for his weary mind, body, and spirit. On his last trip home, he was wounded more deeply by his church, which condemned him to hell for his "sins" of killing. But in that magic moment on Ward Two, he received the forgiveness, blessing, and prayer of an Iraqi man. And it was not just any man but someone who knew and understood, an Iraqi Army officer. David received understanding and compassion. He received in Iraq what should have been found in his church back home on leave. Ironically, he found healing just a few miles down the road from the place of his initial wounding. He found it symbolically and literally from the people he was fighting both with and against.

David didn't know what to say when Aimer finished. He had an inexplicable look. He was stunned and speechless. We all were. But he smiled a peaceful smile. We all did.

We saw heaven that day. We discovered it is not a place with streets of gold or a place where jewels or virgins abound. But it is a precious place. It is not so far away, but sometimes it is hard to find. For some reason we forget the way. It's close by and really quite easy to find. I don't know why we don't visit more often. In fact, I don't know why we don't choose to live there all the time. The Kingdom of Heaven is real, it is here; it is within the heart.

LIGHTS OF THE SEASON

A rabbi, a southern Baptist preacher, and a Quaker minister were walking together across a dusty desert field. Rather than the opening line of a predictable joke, it was the reality of an evening in early December in Iraq. It was a beautiful crisp, clear winter night. It was never totally quiet, never totally peaceful where we were. But thankfully it was relatively calm. The three of us talked as we walked from the chow hall to the chapel. We talked about the holidays, home, war and peace, Iraq, our Marines and sailors. Even for all the talk, there was silence, too.

We went silent as we watched the sky light up. The flares shot over the nearby city gave a festive glow. We were a mile or two away but still had a great view. Like an ancient astrological sign appearing unexpectedly in the Middle Eastern sky, three illumination rockets shone their red glare over the desert darkness. The Baptist preacher commented, "How appropriate! It is the second weekend of advent. Sunday there were three candles lit in the advent wreath." The rabbi noted, "Wow! It is the second night of Hanukkah and so we'll light three candles tonight." The Quaker minister said, "The lights of the season illumine all people, and remind us of the light of God within." We marveled at the unexpected sky show. Together we witnessed a miracle of lights. We walked on in silence, each lost in his or her own thoughts. I wondered who else saw the lights in the sky. Did anyone else think of it as we did? Probably not.

Illumination rounds are used to light things up, to help accomplish missions, to look for bad guys. Chances are, no one else was reflecting on the mystical nature, timing, or message of the illumination rounds shot off in the early evening darkness in the desert near Al Taqqadum. But we did. I don't know whether we were the modern-day equivalent of the three wise men in search of heavenly signs, but we received one nonetheless.

KINGDOM
OF HEAVEN

A TEAR ROLLED DOWN THE YOUNG MAN'S FACE. I don't know who the tear surprised more, me or him. Three weeks ago he'd come here as a wounded warrior, closed off, shut down, and full of more than a little anger. He was wounded not so much in body as in spirit, even though it was the physical problems—a twisted ankle needing X-rays, followed closely by a bout of appendicitis—that brought him here. Otherwise he never would have been flown here from Corregidor, a Forward Operating Base somewhere near Ramadi. The Army, ever in need of people and never willing to let people go, would probably not have taken his post-traumatic stress disorder and spiritual struggles seriously. How could they? Many soldiers had at least some of those symptoms out here. He was nothing out of the ordinary in that regard. They probably would have medicated him and sent him out to keep doing more of the same, day after day, for the next year . . . if he made it that long. Suicide and homicide were considerations. He'd already tried suicide twice. Who knows what the despair would have driven him to this time around? His mind, body, and spirit were weary.

One day he caught me off guard by his openness and honesty. "You have really touched me," he said. "Thank you. I remember seeing you and wondering. I remember thinking, man, that woman seems so happy, so peaceful. I wanted to know more and so I took a chance and opened up to you. I usually don't talk to anybody. But I did with you." So from that unexpected beginning late at night in the ER, every day has been a day of discovery and a day of wonder for both of us. He has surprised me and I have surprised him. One of the highest compliments I periodically receive from people is "you're different in a good way." Some in the more conservative church circles might label me as a heretic. In fact, more than a few at my seminary saw my tendencies even then. But in the crazy, chaotic real world at war, the nontraditional, unpredictable, eclectic, holistic approach to spirituality worked to keep my sanity and apparently touched others, too.

Tonight the three of us sat together holding hands, balancing and connecting our energies together with each other and that of God, and then David and I began to do Reiki on Aimer's foot. David, newly initiated, was doing Reiki for the first time. As we worked together the energy began to flow, slowly at first, and then the energetic momentum built. It was an amazing, nearly indescribable experience. It reached across cultures, across genders, and across religions. We crossed so many boundaries and so many traditional taboos to create a healing space that transcended all barriers and reached directly to the heart of God.

The three of us sat together in that holy moment, in that sacred space, in the presence of God, inseparably linked in the unity of compassion. It was intimate. It was intense. Yet it was a mellow place full of great peace. All three of us felt the power and the presence. All three of us were moved beyond words. We sat in silence for awhile just savoring the experience. All three of us were on the verge of tears. No one wanted to break the silence. We could have sat there for a long time, and given a choice, who would want to go anywhere else? But the hour was late. It was nearing midnight.

What a difference from the previous night! Not even twenty-four hours earlier in the same room were four or five Iraqi police blown up and injured in an IED blast. All were wounded and lying in Ward Three. A heavy odor filled the air. They smelled of oil and gasoline from the bus accident. It was a bad accident. The wounds ranged from mild to moderate to severe to fatal. There was a busyness that filled the air as the doctors, nurses, and corpsmen finished with the final four patients from the fourteen that had come through in two hours.

Last night was controlled chaos as everyone worked hard to repair the blast damage done to human flesh. Tonight, however, Ward Three was transformed into a Reiki room, a place of meditation and prayer, a place dedicated to heart-to-heart connection. Clear Christmas lights, battery-operated lanterns, and tea lights provided a warm, comforting glow. The bright orange, red, blue, and green batik sarongs were colorful altar cloths and were a defense against the dull gray-green floor and dusty white walls. The meditative music muffled out the sounds in the ward next door. The incense struggled mightily against the smell of oil and gas that still lingered in the air. Lights, altar cloths, incense, and music all helped set the tone and shift the energy of the room. Yes, it was a different place from early, early this morning, 0330 to be exact, when the ward was filled with wounded. Yet in reality tonight it was filled with wounded too: me, David, and Aimer. We were all wounded in some way and all needed healing. We hoped for help and took the chance to reach out to connect with each other and the spirit of God.

Like the night Aimer prayed for David, tonight David prays for Aimer. And I have the incredible honor and privilege to stand in awe and witness the ongoing miracle. Is it any wonder I do not want to be anywhere on earth? Most people think it's a crazy thing and in the normal realm, the regular outlook and understanding of life, and I guess it is. But I have found the Kingdom of Heaven. It is in Iraq. It is in a war zone. But the discovery is more than a physical place; it is a spiritual place. It is a place in one's own heart. It is the holy of holies, the secret place where the most high dwells. It is in you and it is in me where heaven is found. The words of Jesus prove true, "Behold the Kingdom of Heaven is within you" . . . And so it is. Amen.

MYSTERIOUS WAYS

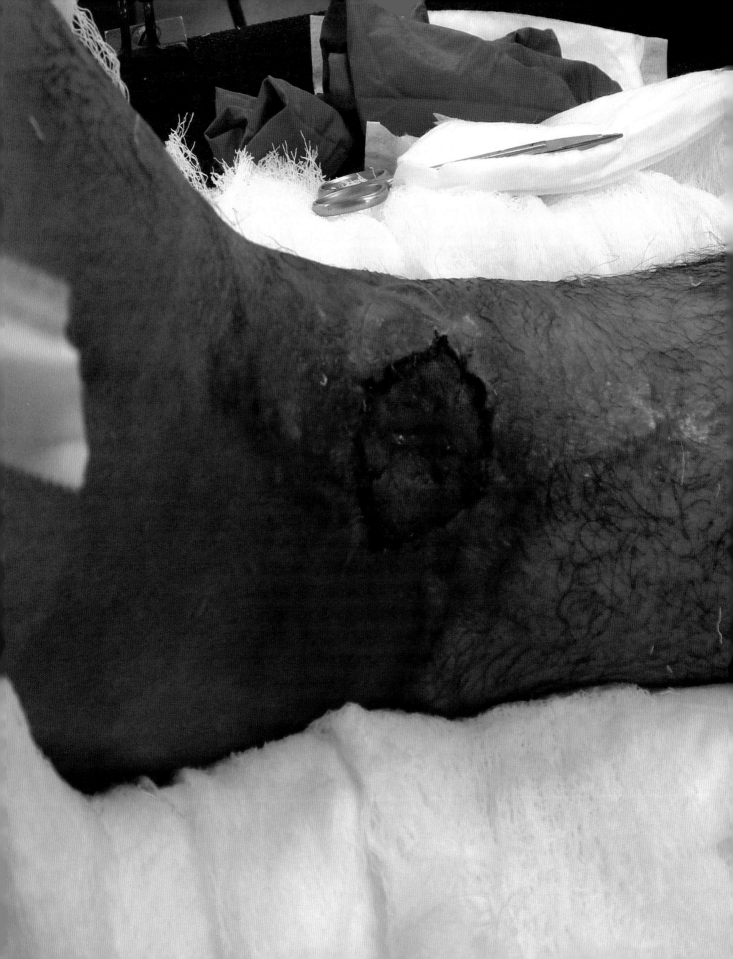

A
BEGINNING

"HEY, CHAPLAIN, YOU GONNA WORK ON AIMER'S FOOT?" The corpsman was finishing his evening rounds, checking and recording vital signs. It was 2100, and he was essentially tucking the patients in for the night. His question was direct and to the point. It caught me totally off guard. I looked at him and smiled as I thought of the adage "The Lord works in mysterious ways." I couldn't have planned it any better if I'd tried, and believe me, I'd been trying. In an instant, I knew and he knew that with one well-placed question he had done what I had been trying to do for several weeks, namely to provide an opening, access, and ultimately permission to "work" on Aimer's foot using Reiki, a form of meditative prayer that crosses into the realm of hands-on energy medicine and complementary therapies utilizing an integration of mind, body, and spirit.

All patient care at the hospital of course was coordinated by the attending physicians, and so if I was going to "do" anything to any of their patients they needed to not only know but give permission. Several nurses coordinated and taught continuing education classes for the corpsmen. Knowing that I was a Reiki master and had used energy work in hospice and hospital settings back home, they had me teach the class on complementary therapies. My newfound corpsman accomplice was in that class, so he knew, too.

The doctors were unfamiliar with the technique and had their hands full accomplishing their primary mission of running the trauma hospital in what was at the time a very busy region of Iraq. A chaplain moving out of the stereotypical clergy role suggesting complementary therapies was not their priority or plan. Yet I provided an easy-to-read one-page introduction to the subject and was more than willing to talk about or demonstrate the method. The doctors had some legitimate concerns regarding cultural considerations. Aimer might not understand and might be offended by my touching him. He could also be offended religiously. Furthermore, he could confuse the technique as being a prescribed medical procedure. So I was not allowed to bring the subject up. I was frustrated, because I really believed Reiki could help Aimer. Nothing else had worked, and it certainly couldn't hurt. His gunshot wound was a souvenir from his time in Mosul two years earlier. It was persistent and nonhealing. It impeded his ability to walk. It impeded his ability to command his troops in the field. And I was impeded in my ability to offer Reiki. I must admit, I machinated and fumed for a few weeks. I was irritated. But I respected the hospital and military rank structure and so resisted my impulse to offer, and I waited and hoped and believed.

And then a sudden unexpected question changed everything. Thank God for the people willing to ask hard questions and to appropriately agitate a situation in need of movement and change. I smiled at how it all happened, because my corpsman accomplice was known as a bit of a problem child. He had his issues with the military and with authority and who knows what else. So the whole scene made me laugh. He had the freedom to do what I had been ordered not to do. He was exactly what

Across the divides of culture, language, religion, rank and gender we shared together in daily communion. Aimer, Chaplain Snively and a Ramadi Cop spend time together and are joined by a friendly green stuffed frog destined to live with Aimer's kids in Baghdad.

I needed right then, someone to ask the edgy question and push the envelope. Thank God he cared and he believed and took the risk. The unsung hero behind much of my Reiki "success" in Iraq is that corpsman; I needed him. Because of him, I did more for more people. My experience in Iraq would have been very different had that one interchange not taken place. Who knows what the ripple effect will be as people remember and reflect years from now on the moments of magic that happened as a result on Ward Three?

It takes all of us, with our strengths and even our quirks, working together to make life work best. I stood in awe. It was a divine appointment. I marveled at the timing. With different people on a different deployment, the chemistry and interactions would have been totally different. It was the right time, the right people, and the right place. There are no accidents. We were exactly where we needed to be for our own growth and for whatever we needed to learn from and give to each other.

Aimer looked at me, looked at the corpsman, and looked back at me. He was puzzled, and so he asked, "What does he mean?"

I took a deep breath, and as clearly and simply as I could, I tried to explain: "I have been wanting to work on your foot using a hands-on meditation, prayer technique, but the doctor did not want me to ask you because he was afraid you would not understand or that you would be offended because I am a woman and a Christian and I would be asking to touch you."

IT TAKES ALL OF US WITH OUR STRENGTHS AND EVEN OUR QUIRKS WORKING TOGETHER TO MAKE LIFE WORK BEST.

Maybe it was because we were already friends and he trusted me or my chaplain position; we had been reading the Koran together every night for at least a month. Maybe it was because he understood and believed in prayer. Maybe it was because he was desperate to try anything to make his foot better. Whatever the reason, he looked at the corpsman, looked at me, and said, "Yes, yes, please go ahead and work on my foot."

I was stunned. Just like that, I had an informed patient making his own decision and request. Outstanding! Aimer understood it to be spiritual, so now it was squarely in my arena; it was now legitimate for me to do. I smiled at Aimer as I reached for his foot and said, "Oh, good. I have wanted to work on you. I really think it will help and can't wait to see what happens." I then gave a sly smile to the corpsman and said, "Thanks, man, you did it."

He beamed, obviously quite pleased with himself. "No problem, Ma'am, no problem." He finished recording the vitals and wandered off, leaving me to lay hands on and touch Aimer's foot. It was the beginning of my Reiki practice in Iraq, the first night of what would become a nightly ritual on the Iraqi ward.

HONORED
AND AMAZED

M Y HEART IS FULL AND I AM BLESSED. "I am the Light of God, I am the Love of God, I am the Healing power of God, I am, I am, I am." My head bowed in prayer, connecting with the Spirit of God, waiting, listening, but more than that, simply being in the presence or more precisely taking time to be conscious of what always is: the presence within and the presence all around. Energy moves, energy flows; there are tingling sensations in my hands and my arms, and surges of energy jolt through my body from head to toe and down my arms and to my hands. Heat builds. The room is warm anyway but I get even hotter as I work, connect, concentrate, meditate, and let it flow. In many ways one Reiki session is like any other, yet every Reiki session is subtly different. The people are different; the day is different; things change. I change.

Four people with four different challenges is nothing particularly unusual, especially in a hospital ward. Sick or injured people are trying to get well. Intravenous lines run from the patients to the bags hanging above; stainless-steel sinks equipped with antibacterial soap and paper towels nearby are in each room. There is a TV to pass the time, and a few clothes and books are stacked on a table or chair. Pictures decorate the otherwise sterile walls. Patients talk on the phones or look at magazines. Typical stuff; it's a hospital. At first glance there is nothing unusual, until one looks just a little closer. . . .

There are two open-bay hospital wards, each able to accommodate eight patients. The freshly painted walls cover rough plywood; the concrete floor is painted a steel gray; the beds are really aluminum-frame cots covered with green canvas; the tables and chairs are an odd conglomeration of white plastic patio furniture, folding chairs, desk chairs, and wooden picnic-table benches made from unfinished scrap lumber. The IV bags hang from cords strung along the wall. The pictures on the walls were not selected by an interior designer but instead are drawings by American schoolchildren. The television has limited programming that given time loops again and again and again from movies to news to sports and back again, 24/7, nonstop. The workers mix and mingle with the patients, eating, talking, watching TV, sitting around playing cards, or sharing snacks together, nutritious ones like M&Ms, Ding Dongs, nuts, cookies, or sugary cereals. The TVs and the DVDs sometimes compete from ward to ward. Sometimes they compete even within the same one.

After working on Aimer, I offered to work on the others. I think at first he was a little reluctant to share the offer, but he did. The other guys took me up on the offer, probably because they'd watched me working on Aimer for the last few days. Not only do they want the attention and care, but they want healing, too. They've heard Aimer's testimony directly from him. Aimer's foot is truly amazing. The difference is astounding. He is finally healing after two years. He gives all the glory to God. His foot tonight was smoking with energy; last night it was too, so different from when I started on him in December when it felt dead, without energy. He and I believe along with some of the nurses that the Reiki, the meditative prayer, and Aimer's strong faith have combined to change what was a stubborn, nonhealing wound. Before one of the guys from Aimer's battalion left yesterday or the day before, he asked Aimer to tell me, "Thank you, you are a good Imam, you are faithful and come to see us."

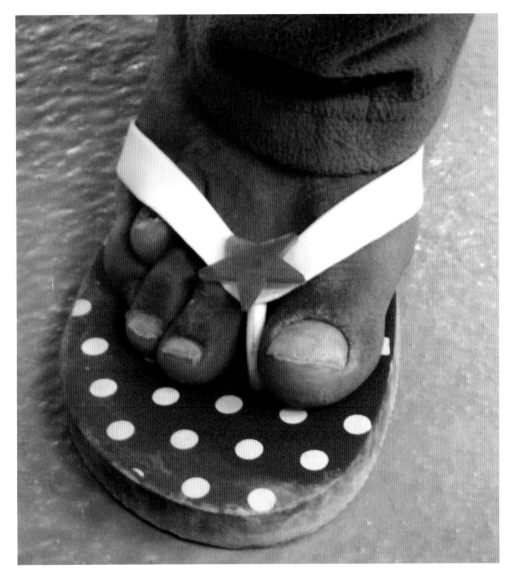

The foot in the myriad of shapes, sizes and conditions became symbolic of the hope for forward movement and progress in a new Iraq. It also symbolizes how I served many of the Iraqi patients who came through the hospital. Much of my Reiki (energy work/meditative prayer) was on foot injuries.

I worked on a guy hit in the knee who'd had a four-hour surgery earlier in the day. There was a lot of energy in his knee, a lot of heat. He told Aimer after the Reiki treatment that there was less pain and that he felt better. A guy with a foot injury wanted me to work on him, too. He was very cute, younger than the rest, and he looked more European. He had a casual *GQ* look with his stylish glasses, sporty haircut, and collared T-shirt. His foot felt incredibly energetic. I had jolts of energy moving through me as I worked on him. But beyond the physical indications, the energy gave me an interesting metaphysical insight. Many foot injuries come through here. Many Iraqis shoot themselves in the foot, maybe on purpose, maybe not. But the message became clear and incredibly symbolic. And so my prayer became, "Heal this foot. Heal the feet. Heal these men so they can stand strong and move and take steps forward. Help them take the steps they need to for themselves and their people, their country, its healing, strength, protection, progress."

David wandered back about this time and was standing behind me as I was giving my insight to Aimer. He and Aimer nodded in agreement, and Aimer translated and shared my prayer with his Iraqi army buddies. They nodded in agreement and thanked me. Before the night was over, I, too, thanked them for letting me have the honor of working on them. I stand in amazement and recognize the miracle. We have crossed cultural, religious, and gender barriers and who knows what else simply to be with each other in the presence of God. As Middle Eastern men they are not usually open to women as spiritual leaders. In a culture where men and women do not hang out together, where women and men outside of a family do not touch each other, they let me be with them, pray with them, and touch them in body, mind, and spirit. Beyond my prayer that night, my word for my Iraqi flock was, "I am honored and amazed. Thank you for the opportunity and for the trust. God is God, the Spirit is the Spirit, and we pray together and help each other."

Aimer translated for me. The men nodded and gestured with their hand over their hearts and said, "*Shukron* and good night."

Patients came and went at all hours of the day and night, sometimes on very little notice, so I asked Aimer to tell them that if they were gone tomorrow before I came to visit, I would indeed miss them. He did, and they nodded and smiled.

David is still in turmoil. He is still waiting, but he seems more mellow. He, too, I think, is doing better with the care and compassion and attention from all the staff, and he likes the Reiki. He is deepening and thinking about his own spiritual journey.

PAYING
BACK

"I'M NOT LEAVING UNTIL TUESDAY. . . ." he said with a pause, his voice trailing off. He had to wait a few more days, and understandably he was anxious to go. He'd been talking about "getting out of here," but now I detected some hesitancy. I understood. I thought back to the night I first met David.

It was a December night, nearly midnight in the ER. I can't remember whether I was doing my late night rounds, was there just changing batteries on my radio, or if in fact the radio had gone off announcing incoming. But what I do remember is that David was not happy to be there. He was hurting. He needed help, but he did not want to be operated on. Yet the prospect made the surgeon happy. Finally, the surgeon got his wish. All day long he had said, "No surgeries today, bad day; a day without surgery is like a day without sunshine." It's good when people enjoy their jobs and want to help. Unfortunately in this business, to use those skills means someone needs a surgery because the person is sick or injured or wounded. Anywhere, but especially in

Iraq, in a war zone, in a trauma hospital bored is good. Nonetheless, David supplied him with the desired surgery, a routine appendectomy.

I talked with David briefly, but he was in no mood or frame of mind to chat. He was busy trying to talk the surgeon out of the operation even though his appendix was bulging and threatening to burst. The pain was making him goofy; so, too, was the pain medication. Surgery anywhere is never without risk, but in Iraq it is even more challenging. It is not the cleanest environment; basic infection control is an issue.

Now, three weeks later, David was still stuck in a hospital in Iraq. A lot had transpired since his first night here. He had a physical wound that wasn't healing well, and we had discovered a guy with even deeper wounds in mind and spirit. Initially he was combative and negative, but he was mellowing. Day by day we saw the change. In a safe environment with caring people, he was responding. It was his third or fourth time here. He's spent two and a half of his four years in the army in Iraq. Last year he watched his friend die. Last year he shot and killed a kid. Last year he tried to kill himself. Last year he reenlisted and volunteered to return to Iraq. He thought he could handle it; he thought it would be all right. This year he knows he can't and it's not okay.

LAST YEAR HE SHOT AND KILLED A KID. LAST YEAR HE TRIED TO KILL HIMSELF.

We talked every day, but today was different. He had a sense of urgency, and the questions poured out in a rush as he asked me, "How long does it take to learn Reiki? What level is your RP [religious program specialist]? Can she work on other people?"

I tried to keep up with the rapid-fire barrage and answered in quick succession, "Usually, Reiki I is an all-weekend course. I initiated RP3 in Level 1 Reiki and yes, with Level 1 you work on yourself and can work on others as well, usually family and friends to begin with."

"I wasn't sure if you could teach it or not," he stated, and then followed by asking, "Do we have time? Could you teach me before I leave on Tuesday?"

Wow! I was blown away. I thought about my schedule. There were some things I had to do the following day, but there was still plenty of time to squeeze in several hours of "class" and plan his initiation for Monday night or Tuesday during the day. I was stunned. It certainly wasn't following the "normal" course of traditional Reiki training, but then there was nothing normal about this place. Desperate times and situations call for creative, out-of-the-box measures. My initial Reiki training was in 1996 while working at Sharp Hospital and San Diego Hospice, but I marveled once again at the spiritual leadings that began in the summer of 2005, while working with the Marines at Kaneohe Bay, and prompted me to pursue becoming a Reiki master. I felt then that I was already becoming one. There were Divine appointments and providential meetings. I met a Reiki master named Jennifer in 2006 during my active-duty stint working with Hurricane Katrina–affected personnel moved from New Orleans to Millington. Her sincerity, compassion, and openness to initiating people as they come to her without a lot of formality and without a high monetary cost was inspirational. I want to remain true to the Usui system and understanding, but I also understand the world's desperate need, and in desperate times I want to be part of the healing. The doors opened and I walked through them not knowing what lay on the other side. I am thankful that I did. It made a difference for me in Iraq. I was initiated as a Reiki master on July 16, 2006 in Memphis, Tennessee, but believe I really became one on December 26, 2006, in Iraq when I initiated my RP.

As the weeks in Iraq unfolded, the energy continued to heal and to draw people. It was subtle, maybe visible only to those who had eyes to see, but there were changed hearts and changed lives. And at least for a few moments there was more love, peace, joy, patience, connection, compassion, gratitude, and trust. All these things emerged more and more in the patients on wards One and Two. We lived, moved, and had our being in the presence of the energy, in the Spirit of compassion.

David and I talked about Reiki. I worked on him every night except one while he was at Al Taqqadum. We talked about energy and spirit. He told me about his spiritual journey by saying, "I don't know, I just like it and I'd like to continue it on myself and other people. I've just always kind of felt like I wanted to help people, to save them. Don't know why I became infantry. I guess you do help and save people, but you do take some out along the way, too. But this just feels like a place I want to go now. . . ."

Yes, absolutely, I would find time, I would make time to complete the divine appointment—to initiate and introduce people to Reiki who are ready and eager, who have glimpsed the power of compassion and who want to follow that way as part of their spiritual practice. What a crazy, wonderful world that brought me exactly where I wanted to be, where I was supposed to be: in Iraq, working for the U.S. Navy.

David and I talked for twenty minutes or more, but the hour was late and he needed to shower, so he left and I went to talk with the chiefs in a nearby office. We talked about all kinds of things, ranging from complementary therapies like Reiki and acupuncture to the latest football stats. We talked longer than I realized, and pretty soon David came back. He saw me and smiled and asked, "You know, I got to thinking while I was in the shower, after you teach me Reiki can I work on Aimer? Can he be the first person I work on, kind of like paying him back in return for what he's done for me?"

For the second time in less than an hour, I was blown away by David. I stood amazed and said, "Absolutely! I think that's a wonderful idea." And I thought to myself, "My God, he gets it! Care, compassion, heart-to-heart connection—an American infantryman wanting to learn hands-on healing and then in turn use it on an Iraqi Army officer in a gesture of brotherly love." Now well past midnight, it really was time to say good night and go to bed. But my heart was wonderfully full and warm as I finally drifted to sleep at the end of another unbelievable day.

EVERYDAY THINGS

Triggers are everywhere in a war. They are important parts of guns and bombs. But they are another part of war, too, part of the after-effects that can shape people for good or for ill forever. Triggers are just as real and just as important in fighting the internal battles that rage after the war. For anyone dealing with combat stress or post-traumatic stress disorder as a combat veteran, or anyone else who has experienced powerful or traumatic events in his or her life, triggers can be serious. A trigger is anything that causes a flashback or an immediate remembrance that transports the person to an earlier place and time, the place and time of the initial trauma. This experience usually entails much more than a simple memory. Triggers often cause one to relive the sights, the sounds, the smells, and the terror. Part of coming home is learning to recognize, understand, cope with, and manage triggers. Although many veterans have experienced the same event in the same location, our experiences are as unique as each one of us, so one also discovers that triggers are unique, too. They come in all shapes and sizes.

Recognizing our own personal triggers is half the battle. I am not currently working in situations where I see the dead or the wounded, so the obvious negative triggers are not a daily threat for me. However, there are peculiar yet mundane things common to everyday life that will forever make me think of Iraq.

Because necessity is the mother of invention, simple everyday objects took on new purpose and new symbolism in our unusual circumstances in a war zone. We took nothing for granted, found creative uses for many things, learned to make do with what we had, and appreciated things sent to us by fellow Americans. Some of the items are iconic Americana, everyday things that will forever remind me of Iraq.

Necessity and boredom sometimes combine to make recycling attractive. Common ordinary things take on new purpose, and instead of being thrown away they have a new lease on life. Those everyday things, however, now remind me of Iraq. RPSN Jappe sits in the chapel office in Fallujah and plays a guitar made from a cigar box.

MY UGANDAN
FRIENDS

"YOU'RE GIVING THESE TO ME . . . TO US? Oh, I can't believe it! Really?"

I smiled and nodded, and said, "Yes, they are yours. Better to be with you, well used and well loved, than sit in the storage room in back of the chapel."

His eyes sparkled and a big, bright smile filled his whole face. Alex didn't know whether to hug me or hug the drum he was clutching. He managed to do both as he declared, "You know, God used you to answer our prayers." I gave him a quizzical look and he began to explain. "We attend church here, but we also have our own worship services and prayer at our compound. We have been hoping and praying for something that would help us. God heard our prayers and used you to answer them. At home in Uganda we drum when we pray and we pray when we drum. Now we have drums. Now we can pray better."

There were a few other guys around Al Taqqadum who were drummers, but they were leaving soon too. My drum circles in Iraq had never taken off the way I'd hoped, but even though small they'd been consistent, usually with Alex and a few of his friends. I taught him some rhythms I'd learned in Memphis, and he of course taught me some from Uganda. He always had a dilemma, though. He was a drummer and a dancer, but he couldn't do both at the same time. So he would alternate. I don't know which I liked better—he was so good at both. I thought back over the months I'd been in Iraq and remembered our drum circles, the time of fellowship, connection, and prayer. Alex and I sat together in awe as we felt the warm glow and connection of the Spirit. We marveled at the unique way I'd been used to answer the prayers of a group of Ugandan guys working in Iraq.

I never like saying good-bye and I never like a good time to be over, and this was not making my last week in Iraq any easier. It was bittersweet. But the conversation took on even more intensity when Alex went on to say, "You know, God used you as an answer to prayer in another way, too."

Still stunned from the earlier revelation, I wondered aloud and asked, "Oh really, how's that?"

He hugged me again, this time even tighter. The sparkle in his eyes turned to a glisten of tears. "No one, especially a stranger, has ever been this nice to me. God told me months ago that someone would come and help me. My mother died when I was young. I never knew my father. I was raised by an aunt. Now I know God sent you. You've loved me like a mother. Can I call you Mom?"

Now I had tears in my eyes. The drums were one thing, but this was a completely different level of connection. My head spun as I was hit with the sincerity and intensity of his words and his request. Now it was my turn to hold him tighter and whisper, "Yes, Alex I will be proud to be your mom."

"Mom, thank you for coming to Iraq. Thank you for loving me . . . for loving us. These are for you." Alex smiled and handed me some packages. I smiled back. They were sad smiles, though. We both knew this was our final good-bye.

I protested and said, "Alex you didn't have to give me anything."

He smiled again. "I know, but I want you to have these." I felt honored but guilty as I opened the packages. The third-country nationals who work hard for us in Iraq don't make much money, and most either save their money to make a better life for themselves or send it home to family members in some faraway land. So whatever the gifts were, I knew they represented a sacrifice and were true tokens of friendship and love. Inside one package was a jogging suit sporting the Ugandan national colors, black, yellow, and red. Inside the other package was a

GOD TOLD ME MONTHS AGO THAT SOMEONE WOULD COME AND HELP ME.

small crystal globe on a glass stand. It was beautiful. I'd seen these globes before and had always wanted one. Now, in the middle of Iraq, I had one as a visible reminder of my trip halfway around the world and my connections with people all over the globe.

Later my mind was still spinning as I carefully wrapped the globe in the sweat suit and readied it to ship home. I'd given so much in Iraq, but I received so much more in return. I even came home with an adopted son.

After I was home, I thought often of my drums at TQ. I could envision them in the Ugandan compound along the right side of road as one headed toward Engineer Village. The thought made me smile. Something else made me smile, too. Alex kept in touch with me throughout 2007 via email and periodically I'd answer my phone to hear the familiar English with the Ugandan accent, "Hello, Mom. How are you?" But the last time I heard from him he said he was going home to Uganda soon. The company he worked for had lost their contract, so he and his friends were going home. I haven't heard from him since. I don't know where the drums are. I don't know where Alex is. Now when I think of them, I smile a sad smile and hope someday to again hear, "Hello, Mom. How are you?"

In many cultures drums are used to communicate and connect people with each other and with God. The small TQ drum circle was a way to relax, celebrate and pray with my Ugandan brothers. Gifts for my friends: Alex and his friends on the night I gave them the drums to keep.

FOR OUR OWN DEAR LAND

UGANDAN NATIONAL ANTHEM

Oh Uganda may God uphold thee,
We lay our future in thy hand,
United free for liberty
Together we'll always stand.

Oh Uganda the land of freedom,
Our love and labour we give,
And with neighbours all,
At our country's call
In peace and friendship we'll live.

Oh Uganda! the land that feeds us,
By sun and fertile soil grown,
For our own dear land,
We shall always stand,
The pearl of Africa's Crown.

The Gospel Choir practice had ended, and our impromptu drum circle that usually met afterward was finished, too. People were talking and saying their good-byes. It was late, but my friends were going to do one more thing for me. Alex stood ready beside the electronic keyboard in the rough wooden chapel. His friend began to play the music with a surety born of years of practice as a pastor's son while Alex's clear, strong, proud voice filled the air.

A national anthem is meant to unify a people and engender pride. A nation's anthem often tells a past story and a future hope. It is part of a national culture and for many, hearing one's own national anthem sends just a little tingle up the spine and brings a tear to the eye. But as Alex sang the Ugandan national anthem, the same thing happened to me as if I were hearing my own "Star Spangled Banner." The feeling and depth were evident, and in that moment of song I united with Alex and his friends as they had united with us. We sat momentarily in reverent silence, but not wanting the moment to be over, I said, "That was beautiful. Sing it again for me." I had him sing it again and again and teach me the words to the first stanza.

The Ugandans are standing faithfully beside us in Iraq, providing interior base security. They are our friends, neighbors, and Christian brothers at Al Taqqadum. I was moved by both the music and the words of their national anthem. It expresses a universal hope. It is truly a prayer for Uganda, but really it could be a prayer for Iraq and for all of us. What a stark contrast to our own battle-inspired anthem, and what a contrast to the Ugandans' difficult history under a cruel dictatorship! As they sang, I listened to each word and celebrated with them.

Together we made music and built a new Iraq. The TQ Gospel Choir:
Ugandan security guards, US Marines and US Navy joined as one.

MY
MANTRA

TWENTY OR MORE CROWS CIRCLED OVER THE FIELD adjacent to the Dining Facility (DFAC) parking lot. Except for the birds above, I walked alone across the open field. Who knows why the birds were there. Had someone dropped food on the way back from lunch? Was there something dead in the middle of the road? I hadn't seen any birds for days and actually was missing them. Life, whether it was a bird, an insect, or a small green plant struggling mightily against the endless expanse of desert sand, was welcome. At home crows are a pesky, noisy nuisance who eat the fruit from our orchard. Here they are like seeing an old, dear friend. Suddenly I was surrounded by a small flock. They moved and swirled through the air, talking to one another, or were they talking to me? One sat like a statue on the peak of the roof looking down and cawing as I entered the DFAC. "Caw, caw, caw," he said. I looked up and answered, "I don't understand. What are you trying to tell me?" He cocked his head and peered at me with his beady black eyes and exclaimed with even more vigor, "Caw, caw, caw."

I said again, "Sorry. I just don't get it." Then silently we stared at each other. Finally I asked, "Can I go now?" He ruffled his feathers as if in annoyance or disgust and glared at me. He gave me a final "Caw." I shrugged my shoulders and muttered, "Sorry," saying it as much to myself as to the bird. I wish I understood. Maybe he was simply chanting.

I have my own chant now. My mantra is: "They come they go, some live, some die." It seems so fitting. Perhaps he was simply joining me in the chorus.

The Ugandan guards stood duty and checked IDs at the DFAC gate and watched the scene from a distance. In some spiritual traditions the crow is a messenger bird, a bringer of magic. Perhaps Ugandan guards understood why I stopped and talked with the bird. Thank God for the birds. I needed the boost, not only for myself but in order to keep doing what I do. We all need some magic.

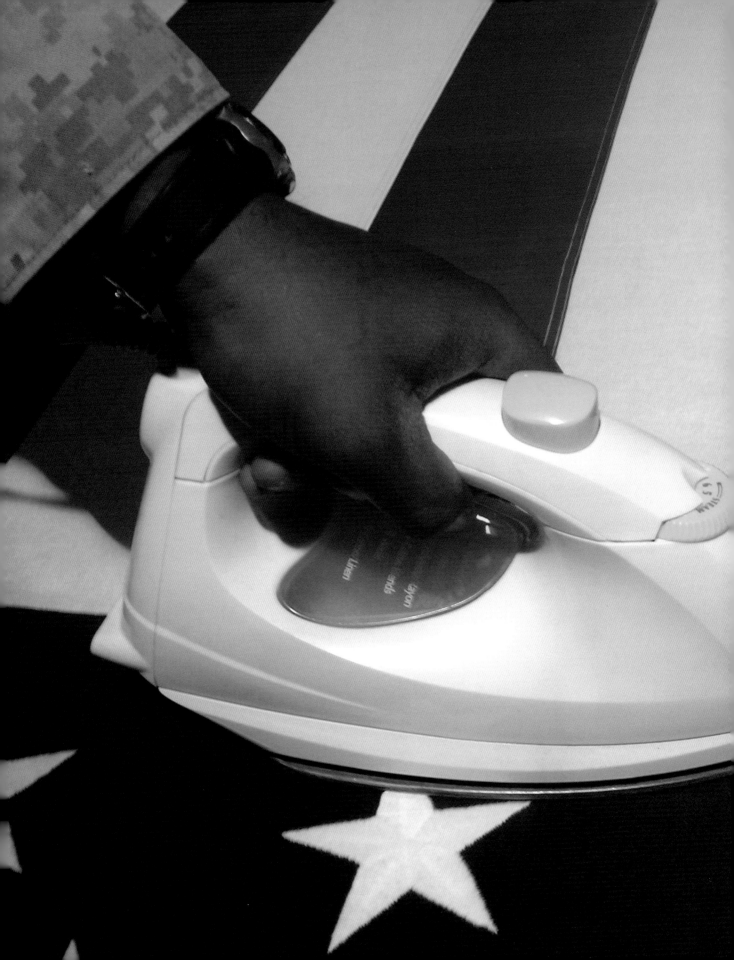

WORD
PROBLEMS

LANSON IND. INC.

CONTRACT NO. DLA-10

DATE OF MFG. 3-85

WORD PROBLEMS

SUSIE HAS THREE APPLES COSTING SIX CENTS EACH. Johnnie has two oranges costing ten cents each. What is the total cost for their purchase of both apples and oranges?

"Mommy, can you check my answers to see if they're right?" Matthew asked.

Simple third-grade word problems designed to practice multiplication and addition in real-world scenarios seemed challenging for me that night. I'd done okay in school, but math was never a favorite subject of mine. Thankfully, most word problems usually made sense, at least conceptually. I could understand and appreciate the reason for the exercises because there was a real-world connection. There were always a few word problems, however, that seemed incomprehensible and unsolvable using the information given. It always seemed as though there was a key piece of information missing. You know the ones: "If a train leaves Chicago at 7:14 A.M. traveling at 58 miles per hour. . ."

I was pleased that my eight-year-old son zipped through the page of simple word problems and I recalled my own childhood word-problem homework. I got lost in my own thoughts, remembering word problems from years ago and then musing on recent ones. Matthew shook my shoulder and with just a little whine of urgency said, "Mommmeee, check my work."

Refocusing to the present, I read each problem. But my thoughts soon wandered again, and the word problems got me thinking: Math problems mirror life. The problems are easy, relatively speaking, in third grade, but they get harder as the years progress. The third-grade problems are challenging for third graders, but the children learn and build skills so they can do the ones in fourth, fifth, and sixth grade and beyond. I looked ahead to being the parent of a middle schooler and then a high schooler and thought about having to check that homework. I'd have to review and brush up on my skills before I was ready for that. The good news is, I have a little time. The other good news is that maybe Matthew will learn it by reteaching me.

I returned to the present and said, "You did a great job. You got every one right, and you did it so fast!" Matthew beamed, obviously pleased not only at his performance, but also because it got Mommy's attention. Active duty and mobilization have made that scarce over the last couple of years.

I smiled back, a sort of mischievous smile. He saw it and asked, "What?"

I hesitated for a moment and then decided to go ahead and ask him my word problem. He'd heard the story once before, so it wouldn't be a total shock to him. But it is one of those puzzling, mind-bending, nearly unsolvable word problems.

"Okay, I have a word problem for you," I said. "But it's a little harder than the ones you just did and I haven't figured out the answer yet. Maybe we can solve it together."

He smiled and said, "Okay."

So I went on. "Okay, ready? It goes like this. . . ."

It's about midnight—a clear, cool, moonless night. Staff Sergeant Rivera and Lance Corporal Alden of the Personnel Retrieval and Processing unit pull up in their tired old vehicle, some kind of green mongrel crossing a truck with a van. The transmission is persnickety but they've been lucky tonight—the old beast cooperated, although it complained all the way to and from the flight line. You never want a breakdown in either direction. The helicopter crew cannot be left waiting; they drop their packages quickly and go. They have people to meet and places to go. On the way back a breakdown is no better, because the packages in the back of the vehicle must be processed, refrigerated, and sent on as quickly as possible. So, back at the building Lance Corporal Beam and Corporal Sweet meet the truck/van and help carry the delivery inside the old concrete bunker.

Inside, the bright lights and warm heater defend against the winter cold. The Marines lift one heavy black bag onto the simple wooden table. They unzip around the

It stands ready for a call we hope never comes. The old jalopy never has to go far but it's always a long trip to pick up or deliver the remains of a fallen brother or sister. The green mongrel cross between a van and a truck kept doing its duty on a wing and a prayer and a little friendly persuasive maintenance by the Marines carrying its cargo from the hospital or the flight line to the Personnel Retrieval and Processing facility and back again.

length of the bag and fold the flap back, exposing the entire contents. Here are their word problems, the ones for which they've been training since the third grade.

Inside the body bag they find one torso, five feet (three left feet and two right), and three hands (two right and one left). What is the minimum number of American flags Corporal Barnes should iron and prepare? What is the maximum number of reports Lance Corporal Gerlach will fill out tonight? Earlier in the day, Corporal Moody prepared four transfer cases with flags neatly and tightly stretched across the cold aluminum covers. Will this be enough for tonight? "March 1985" is the manufacture date stamped on a transfer case. Which is older, the transfer case or the 19-year-old lance corporal now lying inside it?

Most word problems have multiple parts. In order to solve them we learn to isolate the parts. I remember taking notes in the margins of the page, keeping in mind that some information is extraneous and not helpful in solving the real question. Sometimes the challenge is to find what the question really is, without getting lost in the weeds of detail.

"I HAVE A WORD PROBLEM FOR YOU," I SAID. "BUT IT'S A LITTLE HARDER THAN THE ONES YOU JUST DID AND I HAVEN'T FIGURED OUT THE ANSWER YET."

The mathematical questions posed by these word problems are solvable. The other questions that arise are solvable only to a point. Who will get the awful news? A mother? A wife? Where are they? Which parts go to whom?

Those questions do get answered, and answered amazingly fast. People need to know, and so other people who care, fellow Marines and others who work with them, provide technical skill and compassion to help find answers and closure in a difficult situation.

There are other questions, however, that the word problems pose. Why did this lance corporal die now? Why here? There are so many answers . . . and really no answers at all to these questions. Yes, word problems are more challenging to me than ever before, and I can't figure this one out.

A STORY
IN A POCKET

POCKETS ARE HANDY. You can carry a lot of useful stuff in them. They are also repositories that tell a story of everyday life. A mom empties a kid's pocket and finds a rock, a lucky penny, or sand from the playground. A guy empties his pockets at night and puts his wallet, loose change, business cards, and keys on the dresser. Things don't change much from day to day. It's the same in Iraq. Our uniforms have lots of pockets. We each carry the necessities to do our jobs, and we also carry a few uniquely personal odds and ends.

I've seen the contents of a lot of pockets here. Whether at the hospital or at the morgue, pockets are emptied and inventoried. The pockets tell a story for those who can no longer speak. Sometimes we are left with more questions than answers.

I wondered about this Army guy. He was Caucasian, in his mid-twenties. Both his first and last names were very unusual. Perhaps he was an immigrant fighting with us in the hope of earning his citizenship. If this is true, I trust he at least will receive it in his death. He paid the ultimate price for his personal opportunity and freedom.

In his pocket there was a detailed plan for house clearing. It was a list outlining each step accompanied by a carefully drawn diagram. There was a "kill" sheet listing each member of the team and the serial number of each weapon. He had a government credit card, an ATM card, a Zales credit card, ninety-three dollars, an ID card, and a tactical course review sheet dated August 2006. I watched the inventory process and commented, "He must have a mother, wife, or girlfriend." Without hesitation one of the Marines quipped, "Yeah, or all three." We laughed and appreciated the Zales credit card, and the lighthearted moment cut the tension in the room. We always hoped for a few lighthearted moments. We weren't being irreverent; we simply needed a break. There usually weren't many during body processing.

THINGS DON'T CHANGE MUCH FROM DAY TO DAY. IT'S THE SAME IN IRAQ.

The ninety-three dollars provided some unexpected relief, too. It always takes more time when there is money on a body. The process is tedious. Each bill is listed on the inventory by serial number. I smiled and threatened my PRP Marines, "Now anytime I go outside the wire I'm going to make sure I have a lot of one-dollar bills with nonsequential serial numbers paper-clipped with a note that says 'Ha, Ha.' It'll make you smile." The Marine doing inventory looked up, smiled, and replied, "Thanks, Ma'am. But we wouldn't be smiling if you came through here like this. This is never easy, but we don't know these guys. I think it would be even harder if we did."

Although this guy didn't have any, pictures are common in pockets. Usually it's pictures of girlfriends or wives and kids. It's hard to look at the pictures. The faces are happy and smiling. We know they won't be smiling in a few hours. We put the pictures and the other personal effects on the table adjacent to the loved one. But it's too hard to have the families stare at us, especially when their images are stained with blood. We turn them face down.

The Marine was almost done with the inventory. The only things left were a bloody ripped glove and an American flag patch, a unit patch, and a name badge that were strewn across the table; the other remnants of his uniform were still under his bare, battered body. Two other Marines finished documenting the damage to the body. They bagged, tagged, and stowed him. We prayed over the flag draped remains. The process was complete. Now he just waited for his flight through Kuwait, via Germany and into Dover. He'd be home soon.

Normally we never know what happens once patients or bodies leave Al Taqqadum. But a few days later, an article in the *Stars and Stripes* caught my attention. I noticed the unusual name and realized it was our Army guy from a few nights earlier. It was a short article buried deep in the middle of the paper, but it held an incredible amount of information. Much of the mystery about our Army brother was answered. He was a first-generation American citizen, an immigrant from somewhere in the former Soviet Union who came to the United States when he was ten or twelve years old. My eyes welled with tears as I remembered that night at PRP. We knew that night there was a story

IT'S HARD TO LOOK AT THE PICTURES. THE FACES ARE HAPPY AND SMILING.

he held close to his heart in the chest pocket of his uniform. Now, amazingly, it unfolded before me as a bittersweet tale of love found and now lost. Within hours of the blast, the family received the death notification. Later that same day his girlfriend received a package. It was an engagement ring with a note, "Will you marry me?"

HIS LADY

Dark strands of hair caught the light, glistened, and fell gently across her shoulders and teased her bare breasts. The smooth, sultry outline of her sleek half-naked body was clearly visible. What covering she had over the rest of her was in deep blues and greens. She was his girl. On any other day she looked serene, a quiet beauty with a hint of seductress thrown in, but today was different. From this day on, perhaps neither he nor she would ever be the same.

Now she was hurt and he was as helpless as she, maybe more so. Blood ran from the side of her head. She had been caught in the crossfire, an unintended victim of a war that was not hers. They lay motionless, and only time would tell if either or both of them would make it.

The doctors worked long and hard trying to patch his wounds. They did what they could for her, too. They packed fresh gauze in her head wound to stop the bleeding. They did the same for the wounds that ran the length of her body. Besides her severe head wound, she must have had at least three other deep holes running along the left side of her body. She would never again be picture-perfect. Would he still love her, or would her disfigurement remind him of that horrible day?

Friends and co-workers gathered around to hope and pray. They knew without a doubt that he and his girl would proudly wear their scars together, survivors of a close call with death. She would always be his lady—the lady of a tenacious warrior, he a SEAL team member and she the mermaid tattoo on his muscular left arm.

ROAST
PORK

ROAST PORK LOIN SOUNDED LIKE A GOOD CHOICE, along
with a small salad and a "California" veggie mix of broccoli, cauliflower, and
carrots. You couldn't get much healthier than that. The food at Al Taqqadum was
good. Of course, not everything was wonderful all the time. But let's face it: nowhere
is perfect. It was so much better than what I'd expected, and it was so much better
than what some of our guys had available just a few miles down the road at the combat
outposts. It certainly was better than what most of the locals have just outside the
wire. There was a T-shirt for sale in the exchange on base that said, "I survived the
DFAC at TQ." I never understood the sentiment; I guess some people always need to
find something to complain about and as any institutional food service worker can
attest, the "cafeteria food" is always a prime target for bellyaching.

But as the old saying goes, "the proof is in the pudding." Lots of people gain
weight here; it takes willpower and lots of working out to do otherwise. There are

many surprises in Iraq. One of the first and most noticeable in the chow hall was the pyramid of upside-down ice-cream cups stacked high atop the counter at the back of the room. The familiar Baskin-Robbins logo caught my eye. Wow, thirty-one flavors? Well, not quite. We were limited to only five or six flavors rather than the trademark thirty-one. The choice was usually between vanilla, chocolate, strawberry, mint chocolate chip, pralines and cream, chocolate chip, and sometimes sherbet. The adjacent topping station was always well stocked. We created our own sundaes with extras like crumbled cookies, M&Ms, sprinkles, chocolate chips, or fruit (usually strawberries in sugary syrup). Fresh bananas were available for splits, several gooey toppings like chocolate and caramel could be drizzled across the top, nuts were there to sprinkle too, and finally a dollop of whipped cream with a cherry on top made a grand finish. Just like home. It didn't get any better. Except maybe to share an ice-cream sundae with my five- and eight-year-old boys.

Besides the ice cream, there was a full dessert bar: cake, cheesecake, pie, pudding, and cookies. Every other kind of food imaginable was there, too: short order, barbecue, stir fry, Mexican, Indian, meat-carving stations, and more. The barbecue rivaled some of my favorite restaurants from Memphis and Chicago. Not everything was served every night, but there was always a wide variety. The dessert bar, however, was always available, three meals out of four: lunch, dinner, and midrats. It would have been very easy to get in the habit of a midnight snack or treat, but I resisted that temptation.

The DFAC personnel, many of them contractors from India, worked hard. They made good food and made it a pleasant place to eat. There were elaborate decorations for every holiday. One night, however, I was not looking around or appreciating the accoutrements of the DFAC, neither the plentiful variety of food nor the decorations. Surprisingly, too, I barely noticed the people. For a moment I was in my own little world. I was tired. I was hungry. I had stuff on my mind. Focused on my dinner, I made my way to the meat-carving station in the center of the hot-food area. Freshly carved meat sounded good. I wanted something other than food made in large serving trays and set in warming dishes. The other wasn't bad; it's just that on that particular night, fresh sounded much better.

I held my plate out just as I caught sight of the pork loin sitting on the carving board. The meat carver had made only one previous cut, serving the Army guy in the line in front of me. It was a full, fresh piece of pork delivered directly from the kitchen. I just stared. A dark, dark charcoal black covered the outside of the meat; it was a big hunk. It almost looked jointed in one area. I doubt that it really was, but on first glance it looked like a knee or an elbow. My mind was teasing me. The dark charcoal top was cracked and lighter-colored flesh showed through. There was a hint of that smell; you know the smell, the roasted meat smell. Most of the time freshly roasted or barbecued meat is a welcome aroma, especially when you're hungry. I was lost in thought. The meat carver smiled. I looked at him and realized he was asking me something. He called me back to his reality and the reality of dinnertime by asking, "How many slices do you want, Ma'am?" He had already cut two while I was busy daydreaming. I gave him a weak smile and said, "Two would be fine, thank you." He smiled in return and handed me my plate. He had no idea what I was thinking.

As far as pork loin goes, it looked and smelled great, but now I wasn't sure I wanted any. Suddenly roast pork loin didn't seem so appetizing. It wasn't the service. Our food service workers were always outstanding; they were hardworking and served with great cheerfulness. It wasn't that the meat was overdone; I could tell the inside was still tender and juicy, and the outside was seared, sealing in and adding flavor. I just couldn't help it. I kept thinking about the piece of meat sitting there on the carving table, charred and blackened on the outside with bits of tender flesh exposed and showing through the cracked skin covering. I had just come from Personnel Retrieval and Processing, or mortuary affairs. My guys had just processed two of our own. Perfectly roasted meat may never hold the same appeal for me.

IN STARBUCKS

"Silent Night, Holy Night" played softly but persistently as the background holiday Muzak. There was a hustle-and-bustle feel in the air, but it wasn't frenzied yet. There was still time, and here people were taking the time to take a break. There were friendly faces in the crowd and helpful clerks behind the counter of the cozy corner coffee shop, a neighborhood place where no one knows anyone. I found an inside table near the window and settled in to enjoy my cup of coffee, blend into the scenery, and people-watch.

It was a cool early evening in December. A tall, dark curly-haired man sat at an outdoor patio table. His eyes were hidden behind dark glasses. He wore a dark designer sweat suit. He had a sexy, self-assured demeanor. He cradled his equally well-groomed, well-dressed dog and sat sipping his latte or mocha or whatever it was. The dog was a pointy-eared black, brown, and tan terrier decked out more festively than the halls in the open-air mall. The dog's bright red sweater was both a Christmas decoration and a defense against the growing nighttime chill.

Tears began to flow silently down the sides of my face. Through my blurry vision I saw images of Iraq. Today the dog looked cozier, warmer, better fed and cared for, and certainly safer than the Iraqi children I saw last December. I suspect it's not much better this year. I saw the bruised and broken little bodies wrapped in dirty, bloody multicolored blankets cradled in dirty, bloody arms. I knew where I was; I saw the dog but I saw the children, too. It made no sense, yet the vision made me want to be back in Iraq, and that in itself made me cry more. Instead I was sitting safely, snugly, in the middle of a Starbucks sipping my mocha and staring at a man and his dog, wondering whether this is what a post-traumatic stress disorder moment feels like. My personal experience and study tells me yes. PTSD episodes are brought on by strange and unexpected or, on the other hand, very predictable triggers that cause flashbacks and overwhelming emotions.

Many people fight their flashbacks and try to avoid or repress them. Although unexpected and sometimes unwelcome guests, I embrace mine as intense reminders of an intense time. Thankfully my tears were hidden in part by my glasses. I moved my head and covered part of my face with my hair. The other side of my head rested on my hand. Someone would have had to be very observant to notice, and I don't think anyone was. People were all busy with holiday revelry. I didn't care whether anyone saw me crying; I just didn't want to talk to anyone or explain the tears right then. I was lost in my own world. I was right where I wanted to be—if only for a moment, I was back in Iraq.

A LASTING
IMAGE

IT WAS A COOL EVENING IN MID-DECEMBER at home in San Diego. I don't know why I clicked on the *Washington Post* website. It's not one I frequent. I like it, but I'm an irregular visitor at best. I surfed the site and clicked on photographs from December 2006. The beautiful face of a thirty-something-year-old woman smiled at me from the computer screen. There were so many bright and vibrant faces, it could have been a modeling site for hopeful stars. It could have been a website dedicated to some of America's best and brightest, its most promising young people, and in fact I guess you could say it is. Most featured on the site are in their twenties, some are in their thirties, and a few are younger and a few older. Yet regardless of age, there is a common denominator. They were people eager and full of hope, dedicated and willing to work hard. Unfortunately there is no more hope for them; their dreams were cut short.

These are the faces of the fallen, those killed in our long war in Afghanistan or Iraq. But for me they are no longer just names and faces of unfortunate fellow Americans sacrificed on a faraway battlefield. Now and forever, it is personal. I shared moments with some of them in Iraq. These were men and women I saw as they clung tenuously to the last thread of life; I saw some gasp and gurgle their last breath. I saw others in the aftermath of catastrophic blast and burn injuries. Mercifully, it was obvious that death for many of those was instantaneous; of others I wasn't so sure. Those were hard.

Christmas music played softly in the background of my home office and I was taking a break from the required preparations for the upcoming holiday frenzy. I was unprepared for what happened next. Tears began to roll down my face and I began to sob. Suddenly I was no longer in my cozy Southern California home but instead inside an old, cold concrete bunker building in the middle of Iraq on a cool evening in mid-December. Exactly to the day, one year earlier I met this young, vibrant woman . . . well, sort of.

It was near midnight when the remains arrived. The PRP personnel began the processing procedure, preparing our sister for her final ride home. The black human remains pouch was unzipped and the body exposed. She was the first female Marine Corps officer killed in action, a reservist who'd worked in civil affairs. We learned more later. From all accounts, she loved her job, and it showed. She didn't have to be there; she'd volunteered for her second tour. But that night the worst imaginable happened. She and a soldier riding in a Humvee were hit with an improvised explosive device. The outcome was catastrophic.

The pungent stench of burned flesh filled the air and overpowered my nostrils. The visual image was no better. The body was burned beyond recognition, but that was not unusual. A burning Humvee doesn't give human flesh many other final options. Watching the process was never easy, but this time it was especially hard. Perhaps it was because she was a female officer and we were the same rank. Perhaps it was because she was a reservist. Perhaps I simply connected with something deeper. Who knows?

Those of us working that night talked quietly and wondered out loud. We hoped she'd died instantaneously, but we couldn't be sure. She had been sitting in the Humvee, so it was possible that her body simply arrived at our place in the same position. Yet we noticed it looked as though she was in a quasi-fetal position, almost as if she had tried to shield herself from the onslaught of the flames. Those fires are so intense that the horror would not last long, but long enough to seem like an eternity in the moment. We shuddered at the thought and tried not to think it. But it was too late.

Her fellow Marines carefully searched her body, just as they did for everyone. It was a double-check to make sure weapons and explosives were removed before handling the body. One Marine moved the metal detector across the top of the remains while a second one searched the folds of fabric or flesh when the warning sounded. "Beep, beep . . . BBBEEPP," the metal detector squawked. Moving in tighter and tighter circles above the body, they honed in on the location. Lifting an arm, they discovered the dangling heavy black spiral communications cord, the connection with the radio and each other inside the Humvee. Wisps of the officer's hair were unburned and still wound around and caught in the cord. I wondered what they'd been talking about.

The metal detector beeped me out of my midnight musing. They got another warning, this time from a pocket. The Marine reached in and retrieved the melted, charred remains of a small digital camera. Although damaged, it was in better shape than one might have expected. The find sent me back to my daydreams. As a photographer, I hoped the camera would make it home with the body and that someone back in the United States could retrieve those final photos. I wondered what her last picture was. Was she shooting when the blast occurred? Was it a street scene in and around Fallujah? Was it Christmas decorations on the base? Was it the curious faces of Iraqi children, or the warm smiles of friends and co-workers? I still wonder, and I hope that friends and family received a final gift, a bit of magic, a moment captured in time.

Looking at the lasting images on the website, I smiled back at them through my tears and whispered, "Merry Christmas."

WRAPPING PACKAGES

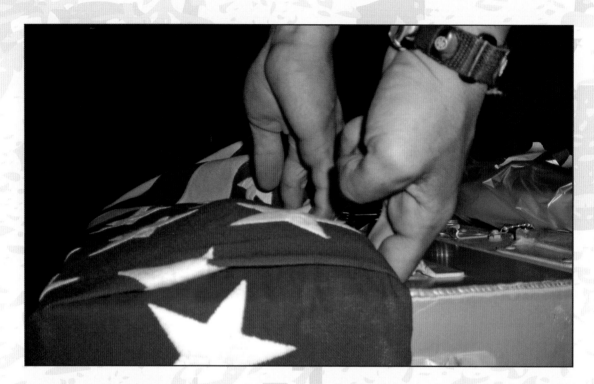

It's December, and packages begin to arrive in the mail, sent from home with love. They've been wrapped with care. We smile at the homemade cookies and drawings from school kids. In return, we buy gifts at the little shops and send them home. We hope they'll arrive in time for the holiday celebrations. No matter where you are in the world, as the holidays approach, no one escapes wrapping packages. It's all part of the ritual. The unwrapped packages will soon be neatly tied with brightly colored paper and bows. Time invested wrapping will be lost in a moment as packages are ripped open in a frenzy. The holidays draw near and anticipation builds. Who does not love to see the reaction on the faces of those they love as they receive the gifts carefully selected and wrapped just for them? Wrapping packages can be fun, tedious, stressful, or hurried. Some people wrap packages alone, some together; some hire others to do it, and some work late into the night.

We wrap a lot of packages here every day and all year long. There is no special season. We wrap them together as a group, usually late at night or very early in the morning. Our packages are all very heavy. It always takes more than one person to lift one. Once the packages are in place, each person has a different job. One readies the unwrapped packages and lays them on a table within easy reach. One carefully checks and double-checks and records their contents. The insides are not the pretty part of the packages but can be striking, even startling. Another person prepares the wrapping material itself. Our packages are wrapped in several layers. The first layer usually is green with a shimmery silver on one side. Sometimes it's just green. It's not a Christmas green, though. It's that tedious, every-day-the-same green: green clothes, green equipment, green gear, green blankets. You can't escape from the green. Not even our packages escape the green. Green is a nice color, but I'm tired of green.

The middle layer is full of contrast. It is a jet-black wrap held with white ties. There are always three white ties holding the packages in place, one at the top, one at the middle, and one at the bottom. All of that is a pre-packaging. Only then, once it's double-wrapped, do we put the package in its box. We use nice, sturdy silver boxes. The silver isn't shiny, though; it is subtle and muted. There is a lot of silver and green in our wrapping. Silver and green are nice colors, especially at Christmas.

After the green, silver, black, and white layers, our packages receive the final touch. It's what the world sees (or now that they are allowed). While I'm tired of green and the dusty silver color, I hope I never tire of the final layer. The outer wrapping is very colorful. Family and friends like it. In fact they expect it, and we wouldn't have it any other way. The final layer takes a lot of time

to get it just right: pressing, folding, tucking, and smoothing. It has to be just right. Too loose and it won't stay in place; too tight and you can't get it wrapped. Our packages all look the same when we're done, but that's okay—they all look so nice. The wrapping is a very sturdy cotton cloth. Lovely red and white stripes run the length of the box. On the top left side there is a beautiful dark-blue field covered with white stars.

Many of our packages will never be opened by family and friends. That's okay. It has to be that way. People already know what's inside. They don't need to see the contents; they can't. The pretty box has to be enough now. We wrap our packages and send them home with love and care. But no one ever smiles. Even with all our work and though they look beautiful, nobody ever wants to receive one of our packages.

COMING HOME

ON THE
MAINE LINE

O N AN EARLY MORNING only two days into the month of February, I looked out the window of the plane at the Maine coastline covered in snow and ice. The scene warmed me. There were hills and trees. Two-story houses formed a dot-to-dot pattern across the landscape. Smoke rose from the chimneys of the homes and the stacks of local industry. Each curling plume gave evidence that someone was awake this early winter morning.

Would the people of Maine be here to greet us? The plane landed, and we walked corridor after winding corridor as we made our way from Gate 6. Finally we rounded the last corner and the passageway opened into the international airport terminal at Bangor. In the distance down the long sloping hallway, I could see shops sparkling with lights and goodies for sale: gift shops, a bookstore, a coffeehouse. But then the best sight of all came into view. There he was: an old gray-haired man, bent and leaning on a cane, standing midway down the passageway, front and center such that no one got by him without shaking his hand. My heart soared. They were here!

The people of Maine were here to greet us and welcome us home. I smiled, my eyes welling with tears. There he stood, as tall and proud as his eighty-some-odd years would allow. "Welcome home. Job well done." He said it with warmth and enthusiasm as each of us passed by his post. His World War II baseball cap told his story—you've seen the kind, with the WWII–era ribbons embroidered on the front and "WWII Veteran" lettered neatly above and below. He'd been there. Exactly where, who knows? Which branch, who knows? None of that matters now. What matters is the warm embrace of one who knows. He'll never know this, but in that moment he greeted me for my daddy.

I wondered whether he was the lone greeter that morning. But then I saw the others forming a gauntlet. The Maine Troop Greeters were there! I was so excited. I felt just like a five-year-old on Christmas morning. These were men who had served in World War II, Korea, or Vietnam; each had his own war, each his own experience. There were battles on the sea and in the air, on the ground in the jungles and in other far-flung places seemingly godforsaken then and now largely forgotten by everyone except those who served there. Names like Guadalcanal, Puson, Inchon, or Da Nang mean something deeply personal to them, the same way the names of places like Fallujah, Ramadi, Habbaniyah, or Al Taqqadum now hold meaning for me. The names and places are different, even the experiences themselves in ways are very different, yet warrior to warrior there is a bond that transcends time.

THE FOUR ARMY GUYS COULDN'T FEEL THE WARMTH OF A PHYSICAL EMBRACE ANYMORE. THEY WERE EMBRACED NOW INSTEAD BY THE ICY ARMS OF DEATH.

I had always heard about the troop greeters. Would they be there for us today? It was awfully early on a cold February morning in Maine so I didn't want to get my hopes too high only to be disappointed. Yet as I rounded the corner there he was, the first person we saw: the most welcome and anticipated sight of home an old eighty-something-year-old WWII veteran, the oldest Maine troop greeter there that morning.

We talked and laughed. We didn't swap sea stories, though. I was a little surprised at that, but there was not a lot of time and there were a lot of people to meet and greet. And I guess it really was neither the time nor the place to go into the details of the stories from then or now. There will be time for that sometime, somewhere, with someone. The stories will emerge in due time . . . maybe.

My mind wandered back to some of the last remains I watched processed at Personnel Retrieval and Processing before leaving TQ just a few days earlier. They were four Army guys who wouldn't be receiving a hug from the old World War II guy standing in the passageway in Maine. Dammit! Yes, they were home now. They, too, had received a homecoming welcome—just not the kind they had hoped for. There was no warm embrace for them. Instead, loved ones probably wept and embraced one another. No, the four Army guys couldn't feel the warmth of a physical embrace anymore. They were embraced now instead by the icy arms of death. Their arms were gone, and so were their legs. The four were a jumble of parts mixed with each other; working together in life, they were inseparable even in death. One bag had one left

Everybody in the military keeps statistics and the Maine troop greeters are no different. One of the first smiling faces of home, the greeter stands in front of her stats board. Day or night, snow or sunshine, they are there for us. They thank us for our service and I thank them for theirs!

foot and two right feet. The arms were mangled and dangled by threads or completely detached. The arms weren't very useful for embracing anymore.

After the short refueling and pit stop we loaded back onto the plane. I returned to my window seat near the front. I sat alone in the row. The serene early winter morning was haunting in its beauty. It was peaceful and comforting but also lonely and desolate, even depressing in a way. My eyes welled with tears. Those Army guys should have been coming home in a few months to shake hands with the old Army guys that stand duty here. But they never will. I let the tears flow unabated down my cheeks.

In Bangor, Maine, there were no fancy words, no fancy speeches, no fancy setup, no news coverage waiting for us. There were just everyday people with everyday cookies, muffins, and cell phones. But what they had was more than everyday understanding and more than everyday gratitude. Without ever telling them the story, I knew that they knew. Someone here knows that standing in an old concrete bunker in the middle of the night, in the middle of the heart of Iraq, watching young Marines process four bodies of fallen Army brothers for the long trip home somehow mattered.

I wonder a lot. In Iraq there were many nights when I wondered. The sights, the sounds, the smells of death lingered as I walked alone along the dusty desert roads of TQ from the PRP compound to my little "tin can." Some nights the desert floor was awash with the soft glow of a full moon. Other nights it was so dark it was hard to see your own hand in front of your face. Yet I was always thankful I still had a hand I couldn't see!

Still, on other nights it was hard to see anything but the images of the dead dancing in my mind. On nights like that, the depth of the darkness engulfed me in a strangely comforting, deep intimacy. There was no use fighting the embrace. It was, after all, a death grip. That darkness was a strange place, a refuge. It brought a small reminder that any day, any of us could be the ones lying on the tables being worked on, being processed. In that recognition was a connection with the dead themselves. Not repulsed by their condition, nor running from it, I was brought to a closer communion with our dead brothers. On other nights the darkness was an oppressive terror, overwhelming, smothering, trying to suck the very life out of those still living, those of us who were standing vigil with the dead. Yet even in the midst of despair on nights like that, the myriad of stars sparkled, giving pinpoint glimmers of hope in an otherwise infinite expanse of black night sky. Most nights the moon cast her light, touching each of us with a soft embrace of hope. I always greeted the moon with a smile and with gratitude. Somehow she always lifted my spirits on those dark nights. But I knew, too, that soft light could be a mixed blessing in a battle zone. I always hoped that the beautiful moonlit nights would not portend more business for us.

I thought about the moon. She casts her light, her glow on each of us. We do not own her, nor possess her. She gives her light freely. We share it equally. Why can't we do so in other ways? The fact remains that we're at war and the old warriors welcomed me home today. And I was touched more deeply than I ever could have imagined.

THE DESERT
ROAD

T HE ROAD STRETCHED AHEAD LIKE A GRAY-BLACK RIBBON, as far as the eye could see. Just outside town, houses lined the main street. They were worn by windblown sand and the hot desert sun. The people in the front yards doing their tasks looked worn and windblown, too. They looked tired, and the buildings were dilapidated. Paint peeled from walls, and the outbuildings were swaybacked and collapsing after years of neglect. Sheep wandered in the front yards and grazed between the cars that had long ago quit running. Women hung laundry out to dry.

One desert day was cool. Misty rain fell and the road was dotted with puddles. It was December in Iraq. The other desert day showed hints of spring: a clear blue sky full of puffy white clouds. It was March in New Mexico. On both days the radio was blasting. One day it blared important information; the other day it alternated between classic rock, country, and a sensual collection of modern flamenco guitar. One day the cars and trucks went east and west; the other day the cars and trucks went north and south, all on their way somewhere—home, business trips, running errands, visiting friends or family, wherever people go.

Both days I was on my way home from a business trip. One was a leisurely drive, even though speeds reached 75 to 80 miles per hour. Rest stops passed by; shops along the way were open for business with friendly people hoping I'd stop. I took an early dinner break at the historic El Rancho hotel in Gallup.

The other day was anything but leisurely, even though speeds never got above 35 miles per hour. No rest stops were possible even when necessary. Shops dotted the road through the center of town, but it was debatable whether anyone would have been glad if I'd stopped. I didn't have to worry about that, however, as the decision had already been made for me. It was not that kind of business trip, and it was the wrong time of day.

We moved through town just after daybreak. Very few shops were open and activity was limited, although a few old men sat on the front steps here and there. A few people wandered the streets. We watched them and they watched us. I offered a wave to a few on the way by. None responded, but then again, they may not have seen me. The glass on the vehicle windows was thick. I think, too, that even if they had wanted to respond they knew it was better not to. Even the dogs that were out were intent on their own business. They paid no attention to us either. It seemed that everyone was mission-focused this morning. Even I had a mission. Mine was to be a good passenger and get home in one piece. We were driving through a city where I'd never been and probably never would be again, so I spent my time sightseeing.

They were two days in the desert not so very different yet so different. On one I was a passenger traveling on one of the main streets of Fallujah, "Route Michigan," the Mother of All Roads. On the other I was coming home on America's Main Street, Route 66, the Mother Road.

Desert roads, whether here or thousands of miles away, can be dangerous. A small white cross by the side of the road in the desert Southwest commemorates a life lost. There are no crosses at the side of the road to mark our fallen there.

The Mother Road embraced me. Her people, her beauty, and the freedom of the open road blessed me. It was a blessing to see, to hear, to feel, and it was a blessing to have the freedom as a woman to go and do, to drive and travel alone. I thought back to A'dab, one of our Iraqi translators. She was in her early twenties and had never been out of Baghdad. Now she's made it a few miles outside the city but is limited to living on the base. Even when women had more freedom in Iraq than now, they still had to have paperwork and be accompanied by a male family member when traveling.

The steady rhythm of the tires on the Mother Road sang to me, rocked me, and healed me. But even it is not totally safe. It is not without its risks. The crosses at the side of the road provide a subtle nagging reminder of that fact. Yes, even on the Mother Road there has been carnage and bloodshed, each cross a symbolic reminder of a life cut short, each as individual and unique as the person it remembers.

Suddenly I began to cry. The tears streamed freely down my face. I hit the seek button on the radio, hoping that would take my mind off of things. It stopped on a Catholic radio station. They were in the middle of saying the rosary. My memory was heightened; something was triggered. Driving the Mother Road, I was transported to Iraq.

"Hail Mary, full of grace, the Lord is with thee, blessed are you and blessed is the fruit of thy womb, Jesus. Mother Mary, pray for us sinners now and at the hour of our death. Amen." "Our Father Who Art in Heaven. . . ." I had whispered these prayers into the ears of wounded and dying Marines and soldiers. I joined in with the radio voices and began to say the words over and over in a mantra-like chant.

I drove on in an altered state created by the steady rhythm of the road and the prayer. As the magnificent desert stretched before me, I saw again the faces of my guys. Some I knew were still alive, others were dead, but they were all accompanying me on my journey as I had accompanied them on theirs, and now we said the prayers together again. In so doing we joined in the suffering of the world. It was the same suffering experienced by Mary the Mother of God, the same suffering experienced by Jesus. As I meditated on Mother Mary, Mother of God, Mother of Jesus, I reflected on a woman who birthed a son, watched a boy grow, and stood helplessly as a man died a death of sacrifice. He died a death she didn't understand, a death that was unfair for one so innocent.

Suddenly it was as if I was no longer driving. I was instead standing with an Iraqi woman cradling her dead baby. She rocked the baby and the road rocked me. The tears flowed. The ribbon of highway ahead continued as far as I could see, to the horizon, to that place where heaven and earth meet. But it really continued

MY MEMORY WAS HEIGHTENED; SOMETHING TRIGGERED. DRIVING THE MOTHER ROAD, I WAS TRANSPORTED TO IRAQ.

farther than that, much farther. The Mother Road in New Mexico linked me to the Mother of All Roads in Al Anbar. Mystically, I was once again united in the Iraqi suffering.

I thought about the rosary—not just the words but the physical beads. I remembered the old Iraqi man who lay injured in the hospital bed. He'd looked so vulnerable and worn. He, like his country, needed help and healing. His old, weathered brown fingers carefully fondled smooth yellow-amber beads as he silently mouthed words.

Many faiths use prayer beads as a way to focus the mind, body, and spirit on each petition. The beads are symbolic. Each represents a need and a prayer sent heavenward.

I thought about my own prayer beads. I have a rosary from Fàtima, a set of Buddhist prayer beads from Tibet, Islamic prayer beads from Kuwait, and an eclectic set I made while facilitating spirituality groups on a psychiatric unit. But the prayer beads with the most meaning to me now are the living ones. My set of prayers beads are the connections made and the lives touched. I think of each name and each face and I remember and pray for each of them, for me, for us. My beads now are David, Damon, Matthew, Mohammed, Nechtel, Aimer, Luke, Ahmed, A'dab, Sumia. These are the new 99 names of God, my new prayers. Each of us is a prayer bead; we are all in need of our own prayers and in need of the prayers of others. We are linked in ways we don't see and don't understand. We are separate "beads" yet linked together in suffering and service.

I cried tears of pain, the pain of remembering, the pain of sorrow and the pain of disconnection. But there was also joy and a connection with a power and flow of the Spirit that was visible, evident, and moving. As it had been in Iraq, it was also in New Mexico. The two roads, separated by ten thousand miles, converged for me somewhere among the red rocks in the desert Southwest.

FAMILIAR TASTES

Sudoku books; Nestlé single-serving coffee creamers: Amaretto, French Vanilla, and Hazelnut; Coke cans, kids' Christmas drawings and cards; romance novels and Maxim magazine, and Baskin-Robbins 31 Flavors ice-cream cups are examples of things common in everyday life that will remind me of Iraq. Each item listed above comes with its own story. Romance novels were often stacked neatly in the women's bathrooms along with CDs or other cast-off items already used by someone and waiting to be used again by someone else in need. The bathroom countertops were a place where stuff was sure to be seen; they were a perfect place to swap girly stuff like romance novels. Some magazines and materials were allowed

and some weren't. But the guys weren't left out. They managed to share their Maxim magazines with each other and occasionally with me. We read them for the stimulating articles, of course.

The well-stocked chow hall was filled with many familiar-tasting treats. Hot, steaming coffee was always better with Nestle's flavored creamers. Near the coffee containers each flavor had its own bin . . . blue, red, and brown plastic cups held just a little hint of home. So, too, did the Baskin-Robbins ice-cream cups. Stacked high on the counter near the ice-cream freezer, the trademark cups with pink and brown dots waited to be filled with favorite flavors.

A makeshift Menorah made Hannukah in Iraq even more meaningful and memorable. Familiar Coke cans written in Arabic and English became the candle holders for the evening celebration. The Christmas season was made more festive and seemed like home with cards and decorations made and sent by school kids from all across the United States. They hung on the hospital walls, in our offices and in our hooches.

Kids' drawings were a powerful repellant against boring walls. They decorated the walls of our offices and rooms (or cans, as we called them), and they brought cheer to the soldiers and Marines recuperating in the hospital.

There is no more powerful American symbol than the red and white Coca-Cola can. The trademark colors and writing immediately identify the product and the company. In a faraway place the familiar can connected us with home, but as if we needed it, the Arabic writing was a reminder that we weren't

there. Every day we passed by the cans in the Base Exchange or in the chow hall. One day, though, we used them in a more significant way. It was early December and the holidays were coming. For the Jewish service members the holidays had already arrived. The rabbi was circuit riding through Iraq and was briefly in Al Taqqadum to celebrate the first two days of Hanukkah. He needed a menorah, but there was none to be found. He used what we had and made a menorah of Coke cans. Now and forever, a common can of Coke will take me back to a small wooden chapel on a dusty desert plateau filled with the flickering glow of small candles and a faithful few gathering to worship God and reenact an ancient ritual that celebrates God's miraculous intervention in our lives.

THE RALLY
IN THE PARK

CANDLES FLICKERED A WARM, INVITING GLOW in the dusk gathering around the makeshift memorial shrine: the boots, the American flag, and the small sign with the body count. I looked but turned away. I couldn't go there. Not right then. I was tired. I was hungry. Maybe later.

The war protesters, dressed in the black of mourning, stood in silence on the Prescott street corner. My gaze met each one. Another protester's nearby posters, plastered with images of the dead, haunted me. "The face of war," one read. Children missing limbs, bloodied lifeless bodies—they were all too real, whether in those posters or in my memory. Yes, I had seen the face of war.

The Women In Black stood side-by-side in a circle, facing outward and holding their signs demanding peace. They looked at me and I looked at them. I wore my "Camp Ar-Ramadi Iraq 2006" sweatshirt as protection against the cool evening mountain air, but I wore it, too, because I am proud to have been there and served and I am not afraid to let people know.

I was a child during the Vietnam conflict. I remember the pictures and the stories of returning veterans being mocked, taunted, and spat on. Now, here I was, walking directly into the middle of a peace rally wearing something that easily identified me as one of "them," one of the military. I mused on that a moment. The people standing silently would form opinions about me, about my sweatshirt. Yet they would have absolutely no idea that I was really one of them too, a peace activist of sorts, a Quaker minister in the military.

I wanted to stop and look. I wanted to stop and talk. But I didn't. I was tired. I was hungry. Maybe later. I was overwhelmed, too. The poster images took me back to the faces and the broken bodies of the Iraqi children I saw. I have held those little hands. I, too, have stood as a peace activist in silent vigil, in silent solidarity, praying for peace at the bedsides of children blasted by war. Underneath my Ar-Ramadi sweatshirt, I now wear a pendant inscribed on one side with the Arabic word "Allah" and on the other side a portion of their sacred text, the Koran, a silent vigil, a silent prayer. Iraq, the people, and Iraq, the place, are a part of me now, as every war is for anyone who has ever been there, wherever "there" happens to be.

I wanted to stop and silently pay respect in front of the makeshift shrine. I was not just a passerby who felt bad about Americans dying. I had held those hands, too. I lost count of how many soldiers' hands I held. The wounded, the dead—I've looked into the faces of many of the nearly 4,000 Americans killed. I saw them personally. I saw their bloody, broken bodies. In a sense, knew each one of them by name. I said prayers over their lifeless bodies.

I found refuge in the brewery restaurant across the street. I'm not a beer drinker; I can count on one hand the number of times I've had a beer: once or twice on a college trip to Spain, maybe a few sips here and there from friends, and then, of course, the two-beer ration at the recent Marine Corps birthday celebration in Iraq. I sat down, ordered my dinner, and started looking at the beer selection. *Hmm*... I was thinking about Iraq. I thought about the Marine Corps birthday party. I thought about the beer. I talked with the waiter. I asked him about the peace rally and how late he thought it would go. I really wanted to stop and talk with the protestors. I told him I'd recently returned from Iraq.

I shifted subjects and asked about the brewery selections, explaining my predicament as a novice beer drinker. He solved my problem by bringing me three small tasters on the house; they were all good. I'd better not like them too well, though, or my low-carb diet will pay the price. Maybe my problem is that I never drank good beer. Maybe it's that I've never had the occasion to really enjoy it.

Whatever the case, I sat at the restaurant and savored the raspberry-flavored brew, the pine tar ale, and the amber ale . . . and I thought about Iraq. I thought about the birthday party. I thought about a few of my Marines who like beer too much. I worry about them now that they are home. My guess is that the images, whether in a photograph or stamped on their memories, will sometimes be too much for them too. I wonder what they will think when they see the peace signs in a park. Will a make-shift memorial move them to the verge of tears so that they hurry by?

I flipped through the pages of a tourist magazine I'd picked up on the way to the restaurant. I told myself I was interested in it. Looking at the real estate ads, I even ran some of the numbers to see whether the properties were a good investment. But really, it was mindless activity. I was still thinking about Iraq, and I was thinking about the peace activists in the park across the street.

I ate and got ready to leave, and found I had stayed too long. It was dark now and the rally was finished; too bad, I'd really wanted to stop. I really wanted to look. I really wanted to talk. It was too late . . . or was it? I looked around the restaurant. I saw firefighters in town for a seminar on wildfires; they reminded me of my Marines and soldiers. I had a hunch, though, that some people from the rally had wandered over for dinner. I saw a couple who had just finished ordering, and took a chance and started a conversation.

"Were you at the peace rally in the park?" I asked. Their affirmative answer opened an unexpected and interesting evening. They didn't mock or harass me— they welcomed me. We talked for a couple of hours. In fact, it led to more than one evening. I met with them and some of their friends again the next night. Twelve of us gathered around the table to talk about war, to talk about peace; they listened to my stories about Iraq and looked at my photos. There was wonder and irony and amazing serendipities; truly the universe or God has a great sense of humor.

WAR PAINT

FIVE-YEAR-OLD ANDREW WAS ALREADY DRESSED and ready for school. He watched as I got ready for work. I was back from Iraq and going through the customary checkout and reserve demobilization process. It meant I was working at Camp Pendleton for a few weeks. My baby watched me carefully. He didn't want to lose sight of me and wanted to approve my every move. He supervised. He scrutinized the tight Lycra sports bra I put underneath my cammies. In his words, it was "cool." He of course heartily approved of the Marine Corps green T-shirt that followed.

It was no ordinary T-shirt. It was a T-shirt like the one I'd sent him from Iraq, one from Personnel, Retrieval and Processing complete with the aces-and-eights dead man's hand on the front and a large, gruesome skull with a crossed rifle and shovel on the back. He took it all in stride. He knows where I was. He knows there is a war going on. He knows people die and knows it is sometimes gory. In fact, before I left he helped me prepare and train. He is proud of the fact that he helped Mommy get ready to go to war. He was a zombie doctor for Halloween and ran around the house for a week or more in costume. It was an unusual inoculation against the visual elements of trauma caused by blasts from improvised explosive devices. His mask was gruesome, not unlike some of the burns we saw. His costume simulated gaping torso wounds, lots of broken bones, blood, and guts, not unlike what we saw in Iraq.

I continued to get ready for work, and he watched as I put my cammies on. He made sure my rank and Fleet Marine Force pin were in the right places. The boots and the boot blousers came next. Andrew is intrigued with boot blousers. He has even experimented with them and put them around his thighs. When asked, his reasoning is clear. He told me with a certain amount of impatience, because it's so obvious I should have known, "Well, Mommy, that's where my shorts end!"

He followed me into the bathroom and watched as I began to put my makeup on. He looked very disapprovingly, even a bit accusingly, and asked in matter-of-fact tone, "What are you doing? You don't need makeup in your cammies. How does that help defend you in a war?" I was surprised at his forthrightness, but then with my little Andrew that really is no surprise. It is also no big surprise how much he thought about the situation or how adept he is at verbalizing his thoughts. He holds his own in conversation and debate. In one way I agree with his analysis. But in other ways I vigorously disagree, and so I said, "Well, I wore makeup every day in Iraq and I think it helped more than you might realize. It was a sort of defense. It helped me feel put together. It helped me feel balanced. It helped me not get sucked into the awfulness of the environment: physically, mentally, or spiritually. There are many reasons, and come to think about it, Andrew, war paint has always been a part of warfare, hasn't it?" He gave me a funny look and shrugged. I went on, "Well, you know, didn't the Indians wear it? Even the Marines today have camouflage makeup they wear if they need to. So why can't I wear mine if it helps?" Even at age five I think he was smart enough to know he'd lost that battle. He gave me another funny looked, shrugged, and gave me a hug. War paint in place, I was ready. We were ready. I took him to school and then went on to Camp Pendleton to continue the process of coming home from war.

A few weeks later we were talking about our day: what the boys did at school and what I did. I told Andrew that I'd written the "war paint" story. He knew I was working on my book and so he understood and laughed. He said, "Mommy, I know why you wore makeup in Iraq." I, of course, took the bait and asked, "Why?" He gave me a sly smile and said, "You wanted to be a knockout." He hesitated and grinned and continued, "You know, in case you ran into the bad guys . . . you could just knock 'em out . . . Pow! Pow!" His little hands flailed in a one-two punch motion. I just stared at him

"YOU DON'T NEED MAKEUP IN YOUR CAMMIES. HOW DOES THAT HELP DEFEND YOU IN A WAR?"

with a huge grin, wondering where in the world he'd gotten that understanding of the double entrendre. I started laughing and gave him a big hug and said, "Thanks, Andrew. Thanks so much, that's great." Oh, my little Andrew, thanks. You help Mommy more than you know! At least for one moment, I was glad I was not in Iraq.

CARRY YOUR SWORD
FOR AS LONG
AS YOU ARE ABLE

"CARRY YOUR SWORD for as long as you are able." The words that George Fox spoke to William Penn about the path to pacifism rang suddenly through my head. Wow! Out of the blue they hit me. Using the old Quaker terminology, they "spoke to my condition." I was having a harder and harder time in my Marine Corp Martial Arts Training Program. Suddenly one day in late December I could hardly participate anymore. It wasn't the physical strain; it was the spiritual strain. I was spending more time journaling, meditating, and doing Reiki. Initiating Katrina, my religious program specialist in Reiki Level I, the night before made MCMAP nearly impossible the next morning; the energy was 180 degrees opposite. Both energies were in fact about connecting with others but in opposing ways. One was full of compassion; one was filled with violence. Although the MCMAP training focused on using the least force possible to contain a situation, one still had to learn all the techniques. The tactics are not all defensive. They lay along a force continuum and are a necessary part of the underlying ultimate and tragic job of the military so often expressed simply as "to break things and kill people."

In MCMAP, I was struck. That of course is no surprise. We hit each other in practice. But I was struck in another way. For an instant, I connected with my Quaker roots and understood to the core of my being what George Fox had experienced. On more than one occasion he was beaten and did not strike back. I had at least momentarily arrived at that place, too. I was not sure whether I could use my newly acquired training even if I needed to do so. I was not sure that I even wanted to. I'd trained in tae kwon do prior to leaving for Iraq and I was two-thirds of the way through my second belt in MCMAP. But in a combat zone where there was so much conflict and violence and killing, even though presumably justi-fied and with the higher goal of lasting peace, I realized that my job was not to add to it but to offer an alternative approach. Granted, some might argue that it was easy for me because I rarely went outside the wire and I thankfully never confronted bad guys except in the safer confines of the base hospital at Al Taqqadum. But on that one morning I just sat in the martial arts tent watching. I couldn't participate. Instead, thoughts swirled. I cannot prac-tice as though I am hitting someone. I cannot practice as though I am slashing someone. I cannot practice as though I am smashing a person's head or body with weapons or my feet. I cannot imagine doing so even if I were being attacked.

I understood the progression and spiritual evolution of true pacifism. I understood it is not a command, nor an edict, nor a doctrine. It may not be for everyone and it is a place one may or may not ever fully reach. But I also understood that like any training it is accom-plished only through intent, focus, and practice. We become what we focus on. I was struck by a strange irony. Surrounded by so much violence, many people here chose to spend their free time doing and watching and playing with more. Some might suggest it is a way of gaining control in a world where they have so little; a video game or a movie is somehow an outlet and an alternative to the uncontrollable violent events outside the wire.

A few days after my spiritual crisis in the MCMAP tent, all eyes were focused in the chow hall and elsewhere on the big-screen TVs. They were blaring some important, big-time fight. There were hoots and hollers and cheers as one contestant bashed and smashed the other in the ring. In the evenings, some people played violent video games. From a psychological perspective, perhaps it is understandable; perhaps they are play-acting or vicariously acting out their current reality in ways they can control. On the surface I guess that's okay, especially if it helps get them safely through the deployment and home again. But I wondered about the impact at a deeper level, the spiritual core. I thought about the cycle of violence: violence begets violence, and it permeates deep into the soul. How does that impact a person now? How does it impact one years from now?

For me, I've already seen one too many blown-up people: Americans, Iraqi Army guys, and Iraqi "good" guys or "bad." The blood all flows red and the moans of suffering all echo in the ER and I ask how long, oh Lord, how long and for what? One can only hope the end justifies the means. I suppose time and history will be the judge of that. In the meantime, like it or not, violence impacts all of us somehow.

"I'm at Corregidor," said the young man.

Its being in close proximity to Ramadi and knowing a little bit about what they do there, I took a stab at conversation and asked, "Oh, do you do road patrols in Humvees or house-to-house clearing on foot?"

He looked at me for a moment and hesitated, then replied with a cautious, "Yeah, house-to-house clearing is the nice way to put it."

He gave me a quizzical look. I'm sure he wondered how I was going to respond and whether I'd take his bait. I did and asked, "And what's the not nice way to put it?"

He looked at me again, deciding whether to really say it. He made his decision and blurted out, "My job is to kill people." Now it was my turn to just look at him and remain in a reverent silence, wondering where he was going next.

I gave him the silent space he needed and he continued, "No, really there's no other way to put it. We can't help it. We don't know who is who." His voice trailed off and he had a distant look in his eye. He was obviously replaying a scene in his mind. He went on, "Last year when I was here I killed a kid. I killed a kid for throwing a rock at me. I thought it was a grenade. That was bad." His voice trailed off again and we sat for awhile in more silence until he was ready. "Yeah, that was bad, but you know what was just as bad? When I got home to California, I went to church hoping it would help. I went to confession and talked to my priest. He said what I did was wrong and that I could not be forgiven. He said I would go to hell for that." His voice trailed off again. We sat again in silence. It was hard to follow that. What do you say? I tried my best by keeping it simple: "Wow! I don't know what to say. That's a pretty amazing story. I'm sorry: sorry you killed the kid, sorry the priest said that to you, sorry you're back here and have to do it all over again." He smiled and nodded. I think he was actually thankful to be sick and in the hospital. It gave him just a little time to rest. He was thankful, too, for people who cared: the nurses, the doctors, the corpsmen, and me, a chaplain hopefully unlike his clergy back home. But maybe he was most thankful for the fact that for just a few days he did not have to "carry his sword"; he did not have to give or receive the violence that ran rampant on the streets near Ramadi.

Perhaps one would say my ego got the better of me as I continued to practice MCMAP in spite of the leadings and promptings of my heart. I finished training; I tested for and received my Gray Belt. Now I understand and appreciate more fully what my Marines do, but equally important, it speaks to me. It gave me a different and deeper understanding. Now, even at home, every day I wear the Gray Belt, it reminds me of my training and the wide variety of lessons learned in the MCMAP tent. I wear it proudly. For me it is a new symbol of the old "Quaker Gray."

DREAMTIME

Everyone has a favorite candy. For lots of people it's some kind of chocolate. But chocolate didn't hold up in harsh conditions very well, so people in Iraq developed other favorites. Favorites can develop for other reasons, too. Everyone processes the horrors of war differently. Some people dream; some journal; some lose themselves in whatever mindless activity they can find; some eventually come home and drink too much or drive too fast; some try to get healthy and work out and get in shape. In Iraq our responses were limited. Sometimes wartime dreams are troubling, even terrifying, but not always. They can be part of the process and can even be humorous. After Iraq, I will never look at a package of Skittles candy the same.

One day a nurse shared the story of his nighttime dream. On this particular night a patient visited him. The patient was peppered with hundreds of brightly colored Skittles—red, green, blue, and yellow. The nurse worked diligently all night long to pick them out of the patient. Each time he'd pick one out and toss it toward the stainless steel container in the operating room, it would hit the container and make a clanging sound. He was puzzled and wondered how his patient was blasted by the hard candies, but he kept at it until his patient was fine. The next morning he told us the story and we shared a package of Skittles together. We had a good laugh and wished the job was that funny and that easy.

WHEN SHERI COMES MARCHING HOME

"**W**HAT IN THE HELL AM I DOING HERE?" I muttered to myself. I wasn't exactly scowling, but I knew I didn't have a smile on my face. I could have been sleeping in or enjoying the local shops and restaurants, relaxing and taking the day off. Instead, I was marching down the middle of the main drag in Ketchikan, Alaska, in a parade in the pouring rain. It was indeed raining on our parade! The locals were not surprised. It's a temperate rain forest, so it rains all the time here except for a few weeks in August. But for those of us working on extended active duty on Joint Task Force Alaskan Road, we were still not used to it. Southeast Alaska was an unusual place made more unusual by the weather.

Everything blended into shades of rainy-day gray. The rain never went away. The blustery wind blew the rain and pelted any exposed skin like BBs. Given time, the water penetrated even our heavy Gore-tex jackets. There was no escape from the rain, the blustery wind, or the unending sameness. One day blurred into the next. The only way we knew whether the sun was up or down was by the fact that the sky changed its shades of gray alternating between light, medium, and dark and back again. Beyond the physical challenge, it didn't take long before the weather affected everyone at deeper levels. Although not unbearably cold, the climate chilled our very souls.

A mile into the three-mile route we were soaked. Seven of us marched in formation near the front of the parade. The Vietnam and Korean War veterans led the parade as the color guard. Some wore uniforms; others wore pieces of camouflage put together with civilian clothes. The flags they carried represented America, Alaska, and every branch of the service. The large flags slapped against each other and occasionally caught the faces of the vets as they were blown by the wind and made heavy by the rain. We followed behind the flags and in front of the Veteran's of Foreign Wars float. The float carried a few World War II veterans and their wives.

Every season from March to September for ten years, the Ketchikan VFW post warmly welcomed Joint Task Force personnel and gave them a place to relax on well-deserved weekends off. But this was the last season for the project. The old Vets at the VFW enjoyed hosting the younger ones from all the over the country. They were going to miss the steady flow of JTF personnel. So as part of their celebration, thank you, and good-bye, they'd invited all of us to join with them in the Fourth of July parade. Yet only a few of us responded and agreed to march; now I was wondering why I had. I was tired, wet, cold, recovering from a serious injury, and at the end of the world on a deployment more difficult than Iraq.

Our little group had never marched together, and at first glance we looked like a ragtag bunch. Our uniforms were mismatched: desert digital cammies, woodland digital cammies, old-style green cammies, and Army digital cammies. But we came together. The Navy Seabee took command of and called cadence for our little formation. We marched well. Maybe what pulled it together was our pride. We were representing our respective services, the Joint Task Force, fellow Iraq War veterans past, present, and future, and we were saying thank you to the VFW.

People were sparse along the first mile of the parade. These were locals, lining the route far from the crowds where the cruise ships docked. We passed the small mall on the right and several restaurants along the way. Houses built on the left side of the road hugged the sheer rock wall. Some were painted bright colors. It was the only defense against the mind-numbing gray. Others over the years had seemingly morphed and become part of the gray rocky mountain and surrounding clouds. We passed the float plane businesses, the fish processing and fishing supply places. Finally we rounded the corner near the hardware/garden supply store. The crowd on both sides of the street got thicker as we got closer to the tourist area.

Army, Navy, Marine Corps pride shines through on a gray, rainy day in Ketchikan with a small, mismatched group of us from JTF Alaskan Road who marched in the Fourth of July parade. All of us who marched that day had either been or were preparing to go to Iraq. Depending on which way you looked at it, the parade was either a welcome home thank you, or a good-bye, good luck send off.

Somewhere along the way as I marched, I made the decision to enjoy every soppy, gray moment, and in that moment of decision something shifted for me. I suddenly saw Ketchikan and her people in a different way. These people were standing in the rain, too, and were enjoying every minute of it. They smiled and waved. Their smiles were contagious and they lifted my spirits. But they did more than smile. They clapped and cheered and yelled, "Thank you." It was an unusual place, so I shouldn't have been surprised by the unusual, even mystical experience as suddenly, although chilled to the bone, I felt warmly embraced by the people of Ketchikan. I had been home from Iraq for two months before I deployed again to Alaska, and now I'd been in Alaska almost three months. Yet I realized this parade was my welcome home from war. I looked at the aging Vietnam Vet color guard in front of me and thought about their homecomings. What a contrast! In that instant Ketchikan became my hometown, our hometown; it was symbolic of all small hometowns across America.

Now I smiled on the inside but a tear or two escaped on the outside as I continued to march. I was thankful then for the rain. Nobody watching from the sidelines would understand why I was crying, but the emotion was sudden and gripping. Those of us marching from the JTF were mostly Navy and Marine Corps. Most of us—the Marines, the corpsman, the Seabee, and I—had already been to war; the one Army guy who marched with us was preparing to go in the fall. So for all of us it was either a "welcome home" or a "good luck, God bless" sendoff.

We rounded the last corner near the tunnel that connected one end of town with the other. People packed the street. Cruise ships were tied all along the docks to the right. To the left the crowds stood on the narrow, uneven sidewalks crushed four or five deep up against the buildings of the historic Gilmore Hotel, Annabelle's Restaurant, and various jewelry stores. Patrons toasted us from the doorways of the Totem and Sourdough bars. It was a holiday party. It was a busy mid-season day in Ketchikan. I didn't think the emotion could get any more intense, but it did. We were not only being welcomed home from war by the people of Ketchikan but by people from all over. Every season, people from across the United States ride the cruise ships into Alaska's Inside Passage. For many it is the dream of a lifetime. It's a vacation they save years for to celebrate something special or to commemorate an important life milestone: a honeymoon, an anniversary, a birthday, or a retirement.

Today the cruise ship passengers from all over the United States and the world witnessed small-town pride at its peak. I suspect that whether they hung over the balcony rails of the large ships or lined the little two-lane street through the middle of town, many will never forget watching a Fourth of July parade in the pouring rain. They have their memories, but they have their photos, too. Many Americans and a few exuberant Japanese tourists with cameras waved and smiled and cheered and clicked photos. Our little formation may be forever documented in the pages of family photo albums or scrapbooks halfway across the United States in mid-America or even halfway around the world.

> I WAS WELCOMED HOME FROM IRAQ BY PEOPLE FROM ALL ACROSS THE UNITED STATES.

Little did the tourists know, but they made the day even more meaningful for me. I was welcomed home from Iraq by people from all across the United States and by citizens from throughout the world. How peculiar that we met in a little town in the southeast corner of Alaska! Times change and wars change, but some things like a patriotic parade and a warm welcome home never change.

It was a dreary day but our spirits soared high, much higher than the fireworks that were cancelled because of inclement weather. Fourth of July in Ketchikan was a celebration of America and what it stands for. But more than that, it was a celebration for our souls; a far-flung island and a little town in the middle of nowhere was the crossroads where Americans and citizens from throughout the world said hello and good-bye and thank you to those of us coming from and going to Iraq.

DEDICATION

To the first warrior I ever knew and loved,

my daddy, LCDR A.W. (Bud) Snively, USN, Ret.,

and to my Quaker mother Blossom Snively

and her long line of Quaker grandmothers.

✦ ✦ ✦

ACKNOWLEDGMENTS

THE MARINES RECRUITING POSTER says, "The Change is Forever," and indeed it is.

I am a story-listener and a story-teller. At any given time we are in the middle of a story, not the novel you pick up at the corner newsstand nor the most sensational recent internet blog but instead the story of our own lives—smack in the middle of the main plot marching steadily, even dutifully, from birth to death, surrounded by the never ending swirl of subplots.

We create the stories of our lives through our retold memories. They can be seen as a set of concentric circles, and the more we have in common, the more obvious our sense of community, the more we can relate. But we all have more in common than we might think. Our basic humanity says we all have a need for safety, food, clothing, shelter, as well as the more complex needs such as the need to love and be loved and to discover purpose in our lives. We ultimately seek the passion in life that will direct us to the center-point within our own soul, where mind, body, and spirit are at peace.

Jesus walked and wandered, lived life, and observed. Then with a spiritual lens, he retold the stories he had learned. Some appeared incredibly simple, some contained the spectacular, but all were profound in the sense that each invited listeners to a deeper relationship with God.

It is my hope that the stories retold here will have in some way touched and encouraged you to enliven your own spiritual quest. But perhaps more than that, I invite you to simply sit with me in awe and ponder the mysteries of life and death and the Spirit. I hope you have seen and now believe that, no matter what, even in a war zone, love overcomes hate, courage rises strong in the face of fear, death has no eternal hold, and peace is possible precisely because it comes from the sanctuary of the soul, from a heart steadfastly united with the Divine.

So how does the story end? I don't know. I struggled to write the ending for this book because the ending is still being written both globally and in my little world. We still don't know how the bigger Iraq story will end and I don't know how my part of it will end either.

My deployment to Iraq has been one of the peak experiences of my life. I would not trade my time there for anything. Thank you, America, for the opportunity to serve you; it is a privilege. Thank you, too, for giving me your time and sharing these stories with me. It is an honor to remember and retell them. And to my fellow service members, thank you for sharing your lives with me. I stand ready and willing to go anywhere, anytime with you. Just say the word and I'll be there.

INDEX